The Nuremberg Nazi War Crimes Trials

A Headline Court Case

Headline Court Cases

The Andersonville Prison Civil War Crimes Trial
A Headline Court Case
0-7660-1386-3

The John Brown Slavery Revolt Trial
A Headline Court Case
0-7660-1385-5

The Lindbergh Baby Kidnapping Trial
A Headline Court Case
0-7660-1389-8

The Lizzie Borden "Axe Murder" Trial
A Headline Court Case
0-7660-1422-3

The Nuremberg Nazi War Crimes Trials
A Headline Court Case
0-7660-1384-7

The Sacco and Vanzetti Controversial Murder Trial
A Headline Court Case
0-7660-1387-1

The Salem Witchcraft Trials
A Headline Court Case
0-7660-1383-9

The Scopes Monkey Trial
A Headline Court Case
0-7660-1388-X

THE NUREMBERG NAZI WAR CRIMES TRIALS

A Headline Court Case

Harvey Fireside

E | **Enslow Publishers, Inc.**
40 Industrial Road   PO Box 38
Box 398   Aldershot
Berkeley Heights, NJ 07922   Hants GU12 6BP
USA   UK

http://www.enslow.com

To Walter Pauk and the other liberators.

Library of Congress Cataloging-in-Publication Data

Fireside, Harvey.
  The Nuremberg Nazi War Crimes Trials : a headline court case / Harvey
Fireside.
      p. cm. — (Headline court cases)
   Includes bibliographical references.
   Contents: Liberating a concentration camp — Would there be a trial of
major war criminals? — Assembling the cast for the trial — Setting the
stage for the trial — The case for the prosecution — The case for the
defense.
   ISBN 0-7660-1384-7
   1. Nuremberg Trial of Major German War Criminals, Nuremberg, Germany,
1945–1946—Juvenile literature. 2. War crime
trials—Germany—Nuremberg—Juvenile literature. 3. Nuremberg War Crime
Trials, Nuremberg, Germany, 1946–1949—Juvenile literature. I. Title.
II. Series.
KZ1176 .F57 2000
341.6'9—dc21   99-050926

Printed in the United States of America

10 9 8 7 6 5 4 3 2

To Our Readers:
We have done our best to make sure all Internet addresses in this book were active and
appropriate when we went to press. However, the author and the publisher have no
control over and assume no liability for the material available on those Internet sites or on
other Web sites they may link to. Any comments or suggestions can be sent by e-mail to
comments@enslow.com or to the address on the back cover.

Photo Credits: National Archives, pp. 3, 11, 18, 22, 26, 33, 37, 45, 49, 56, 60,
64, 67, 76, 80, 83, 88, 95, 99, 103, 107.

Cover Photo: National Archives. Albert Speer, director of the Nazi armament
program walks into the courtroom (through door at right). Other defendants in
the front row are (left to right): Hermann Goering, Rudolf Hess, Joachim von
Ribbentrop, and Wilhelm Keitel.

Contents

chapter one

LIBERATING A CONCENTRATION CAMP

WORLD WAR II—Walter Pauk was one of seven brothers who grew up in a working-class family near Hartford, Connecticut. After he finished high school, he worked for ten years as a clerk for a life insurance company. When the United States entered World War II in December 1941, Walter Pauk and his brothers joined the armed forces.

More than fifty years later, Pauk recalled, "When I was drafted into the Army that was the best thing that ever happened to me, because it took me away from a job that had no future."[1] At first, he saved nearly all his monthly pay as a private—nineteen out of twenty-one dollars. He sent the money to his sister, who put it into a savings account. After the war was over, Walter Pauk planned to use his savings to go to college.

The Army Goes to Europe

Not long after Walter Pauk completed basic training, the Army noticed his top scores on intelligence tests. He was sent to officer candidate school in 1942, when he was twenty-eight years old. He graduated as a gunnery officer and was sent to fight in Europe. Three years later, as a second lieutenant, he was in command of an artillery platoon of 120 men and about two dozen vehicles. They were part of the Seventh Army, battling its way across Germany. "On March 26, 1945," he said, "I led my platoon across the Rhine River on a pontoon bridge." That was a type of temporary floating bridge used because all of the permanent bridges had been destroyed.

In early April 1945, his platoon was ordered to take charge of a place called Dachau concentration camp. He had no idea what would await them. He had heard that Dachau was a place where the Nazis, who had come to power in Germany in 1933, imprisoned people they did not like. But he "did not realize that it was such a well-known and important camp."

As American, British, and Russian troops were pushing back the *Wehrmacht* (the German army), they came across hundreds of these camps. They learned that some of these places were used for slave labor—where people from conquered countries were forced to produce war equipment. Other places held an even more dreadful secret—the death camps, where Jews and other prisoners were killed in gas chambers. According to the Nazis, Jews had no right to live. Gypsies, homosexuals, and other "inferior groups," such as Russian prisoners, were also sent to concentration camps.

The German guards had fled when the first American infantry troops showed up on April 30. Some thirty-two thousand prisoners were found by the first American troops, together with hundreds of rotting corpses. The guards had taken all supplies, including food and medicines, with them.

Freeing Prisoners of War

When Walter Pauk's artillery platoon drove by the farms near the town of Dachau, not far from the city of Munich, the American soldiers saw a strange sight. A number of men, who turned out to be former prisoners from Dachau, were chasing milk cows across a field, trying to butcher one with their knives. The town's *burgermeister*, the mayor, approached Walter Pauk. He asked Pauk "to stop this chasing of cows." Pauk sent two squads of soldiers to tell the former prisoners "to return to the area adjacent [next] to the concentration camp."

The mayor said, "The inmates don't want to return to the concentration camp for shelter." Walter Pauk recalled, "I immediately understood their strong aversion, so I ordered my staff sergeant to start setting up our canvas tents, to make a separate village for the inmates." His platoon asked other American troops passing by if they could spare some of their tents. These soldiers "were all too happy to get rid of this excess baggage. Before nightfall, we had a pretty good tent town set up. The tents were set up in military style, in two long rows."

Walter Pauk looked over the camp. The barracks for prisoners were filthy, with no place to wash. About one-hundred-fifty inmates, most of them Jews from Poland, were in the camp. "They were like living skeletons," Pauk said, many of them too ill to walk. He discovered more than twenty bodies, each in a long cloth bag, stacked at the camp's railroad depot. He thought these people "had probably been suffocated," most likely in the camp's gas chamber.

Pauk's reaction was a mixture of compassion and common sense. "Seeing the people, of course, touched me very deeply." He realized that these starving people, "in their striped pajamas and ragged clothes, were in very bad shape." But the American troops did not have the supplies to feed them or care for them.

Pauk had read that people who had not eaten in a long time should not be given solid food. "It had been months—perhaps years—since they had had good meals," he said. "So, soup came to my mind immediately." He told the mayor that the town should furnish him "every day with seventy quarts of milk, a quarter of beef, some turnips, carrots, cabbage, potatoes and bread."

The mayor and his counselors "were glad that we would have the responsibility for housing, feeding and controlling all the former prisoners. They were glad to provide the raw food." The United States Army cooks added "army stocks of salt, pepper, sugar and so forth. The soups were very nutritious."

Soon Walter Pauk's soldiers found another group of people in a separate building. "These were 104 or 105 captured Russian officers. They were all alive and well." It turned out that they were all generals. "Any officers below the rank of general, I understood, were executed." Pauk had learned to speak Russian from his Russian-born parents. So he was able to talk to the commander, "the general in charge, while the rest of the generals listened." In the meantime, Pauk had identified four doctors among the prisoners. "They were older but were in worse physical shape than most of the other inmates. . . . They had no energy, no desire to help anybody else." The doctors were housed separately, "in the largest, most spacious tent that we had." Each of them was given "an army folding cot, soap and shaving equipment. I wanted to rehabilitate them, to get them back into physical and mental good health, so they could, in turn, care for their own people."

Until the doctors were able to function, Pauk had to

Two of the crematorium ovens at the Dachau concentration camp are shown here. Walter Pauk helped to liberate the camp in 1945.

improvise treatment for the sick prisoners. "One man poked at his leg to show me his ulcerated ankle and pleaded for help." Pauk had the man bathe his infection in warm water twice a day. He gave him some of the water purification tablets from his army first-aid kit. To speed the healing, Walter Pauk also sprinkled on some Sulfa, a drug that he carried on his belt. "Almost immediately, the man's wound started showing the effects of this antibiotic." The ankle was healing.

Fifty years later, Pauk recalled,

> It was amazing how quickly conditions improved. With plenty of nourishing soup and kindly care, even after a few days small improvements began appearing. People were walking about now; before, they could hardly stand. Things were looking up.

From extra Army supplies, the American soldiers distributed toothpaste and toothbrushes to the inmates. They also set up places to wash with soap and warm water. And there were scissors for haircuts, razors for shaves. It had been a long time since these prisoners had been allowed to clean up or been treated with kindness.

Pauk also saw to it "that the inmates were not penned up. We did not isolate them—we gave them total freedom—to roam about a certain area but not to go into town, and to stay away from the farms. This was the agreement we made with the mayor." The townspeople were grateful to the Americans "for saving their cattle and perhaps for saving their homes from being looted." They responded to Pauk's appeal by bringing spare clothes and shoes to the camp. "The inmates were glad to get out of their hated striped uniforms."

Yet Walter Pauk had one other unpleasant chore for the Germans who had been living next to this camp. He "told the [mayor] that [he] wanted the bodies carted away and buried." If the corpses had been left at the railroad depot, he thought, they could spread disease. "Each of these inmates had an identification number tattooed on his or her arm or wrist. Among these inmates were women and girls as well as men. I emphasized . . . that these numbers be taken and recorded."

Keeping Records

Walter Pauk turned over these records containing the inmates' identification numbers to the military government staff that arrived. He said goodbye to the freed prisoners, none of whom died under his care. He had to assemble his unit and race to rejoin the rest of his outfit, which was "perhaps hundreds of miles away at that time." There were still battles to be fought before World War II ended.

After he left the Army, Walter Pauk went to college and graduate school. Eventually, he became a professor of education at Cornell University in Ithaca, New York. Yet, before the interview for this book, he had never talked about liberating the Dachau concentration camp.

There are things that still puzzle Walter Pauk. He wonders what became of the Russian generals. He is also not sure that the Germans who lived in the town knew about the horrors in the camp. "I would imagine so," he said, "but I personally don't know. . . . The trains and the bodies were outside of the enclosure, so they could be seen by anybody who came within a couple of hundred yards of it. So, I would guess that they knew. The trains came back and forth, taking bodies."

There are many unanswered questions. Who was responsible for the terrible treatment that the prisoners suffered? Who could be taken to court to decide why many thousands had died at Dachau, though their only "crime" was being Jewish? Why had Russian officers been killed after they were taken prisoner? Should the guilt be shared by the nearby townspeople who did nothing to stop the mistreatment?

Walter Pauk, now in his eighties, leads an active life. He writes textbooks, goes hiking, exercises, and travels abroad. Only rarely does he wrestle with his wartime memories. At a recent meeting, he said, "I had a strange phone call from a woman in New York. She asked, 'Are you the Walter Pauk who rescued my parents?' I told her she must be thinking of someone else."

The woman insisted that her parents treasured the memory of an American officer by that name who had "saved their lives" long ago, when they had been inmates at Dachau. Reluctantly, Pauk said that they might remember him from his Army days. But, he told her, he deserved no special thanks. He had just been doing his job—what anybody would have done.

chapter two

WOULD THE WAR CRIMINALS BE PROSECUTED?

UNITED STATES—In Washington, D.C., government officials had been discussing the same questions that occurred to the American soldiers who had stumbled on the horrors of concentration camps like Dachau. Since 1942, the White House had been looking for ways to hold someone accountable for the crimes committed by the Nazis during Germany's war across Europe.

The first question—Who should be considered a "major war criminal?"—was not difficult to answer. The Nazi party and military leaders, their police and propaganda chiefs were well known. A few of them, including Adolf Hitler, called the *Führer* (leader), his propaganda chief Joseph Goebbels, and the head of the *Gestapo* (secret police) Heinrich Himmler, committed suicide rather than face arrest in the closing days of the war.

As for Nazi leaders who survived, Allied government officials needed to decide whether they should be given a lengthy trial or just a "summary court martial." Then, how could Western and Russian systems of law work together during a trial? Finally, should the central evidence be based on the testimony of the accused or on the thousands of documents the Germans had left behind?

President Franklin D. Roosevelt spoke out more on these questions than the other leaders of the Allies (primarily Britain, France, the United States, Canada, and the Soviet Union) who had joined to fight against the so-called Axis powers (Germany, Italy, and Japan). He talked about the need to bring war criminals to trial. He said that "the invaders in Europe and in Asia" had been committing "barbarous crimes."[1] He warned them that "the time will come when they shall stand in courts of law in the very countries which they are now oppressing and answer for their acts."[2]

What were these crimes? The president referred only to Nazis who had killed "innocent persons for the deeds of others."[3] He had in mind, he said, the destruction of a Czech town, Lidice, as punishment for the assassination of Reinhard Heydrich, a leader of the Gestapo. It was common knowledge that since 1938 the Nazis had not followed accepted rules for waging war. They assured neighboring countries of their peaceful intentions. Then Germany launched one surprise attack after another, in a new style of war known as *blitzkrieg* (like a lightning strike—a quick and destructive invasion of other countries).

In May 1940, during the invasion of the Netherlands, the *Luftwaffe* (air force) bombed civilian targets, such as the city of Rotterdam, even after the Dutch had offered to surrender.

Then, if any people in the occupied countries did not follow German orders, they were arrested. In France, for example, hostages were executed if German soldiers were attacked by resistance fighters. When Allied troops surrendered, many were mistreated in prison camps. Some prisoners, such as those in commando (raiding) units, were killed without a trial.

President Roosevelt did not mention the Nazi persecution of the Jews. The Holocaust that took 6 million Jewish lives was not widely known about until the final months of the war. After all, the Nazis hid death camps as part of a so-called resettlement program. And, until the few survivors were freed, the victims could not testify.

The War Crimes Commission Emerges

Roosevelt persuaded Winston Churchill, the prime minister of Great Britain, to join him in a declaration on October 7, 1942. They announced that they were establishing a United Nations War Crimes Commission to collect evidence of crimes and to identify those responsible. They said that they did not intend to punish all Germans, just the "ringleaders" who had organized the "murder of thousands of innocent persons" and other crimes that went against basic beliefs "of the Christian faith."[4]

Other Allied governments, including France and Canada, also backed the formation of the commission. The Soviet Union, however, decided not to participate. Instead, it set up its own "State Commission to Investigate War Crimes" to prepare trials for crimes on Soviet territory.

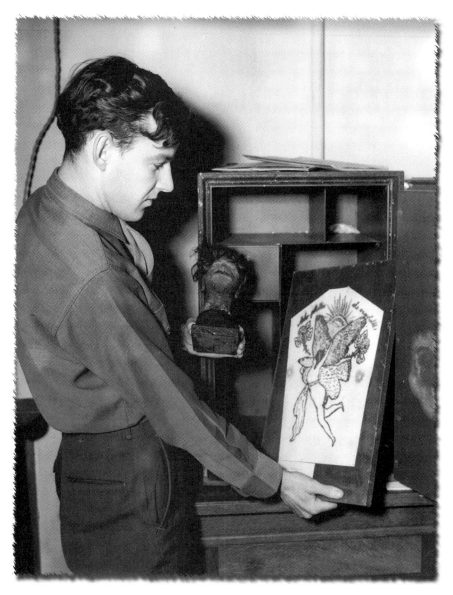

An American soldier looks at the shrunken skull of a Polish prisoner and a lampshade made from the skin of a concentration camp victim. Evidence such as this convinced many Allied leaders that Nazi leaders should be tried for committing war crimes.

By October 1943, Premier Joseph Stalin of the Soviet Union was ready to join Franklin D. Roosevelt and Winston Churchill. All three Allied leaders agreed to hold individual Germans responsible for war crimes. At that time they did not envision one combined trial. Rather, the Nazi party officials and military officers would be tried in countries where they had committed atrocities. They would be punished according to the laws of each liberated country.[5]

Secretary of War Henry L. Stimson and, later, Secretary of State Cordell Hull tried to convince the president that "an international tribunal"—a worldwide trial—should try the Nazi leaders, as outlined in the Bill of Rights, the first ten amendments to the United States Constitution.[6] The defendants, Stimson said, should have an American-style trial. They would be notified of the charges against them, allowed to testify, and allowed to call witnesses on their behalf.

On December 25, 1944, the legal office of the War Department ordered the generals in Europe and the Pacific to set up special units to gather evidence of war crimes. A central War Crimes Office had been established in Washington. But a truly international court would require the approval of other Allied governments, especially the British and the Soviets.

In January 1945, Stimson and his colleagues prepared a letter for President Roosevelt on the eve of his meeting with Churchill and Stalin at Yalta. They argued that punishing Nazi war criminals only after a trial would "command maximum public support in our times and receive the respect of history."[7] All three leaders promised "joint and swift punishment" for war criminals, but they did not yet act on the points of the letter. Winning the war was far more important at that time.

After the Yalta conference, President Roosevelt sent Judge Samuel Rosenman to Great Britain as his personal representative. Churchill told Rosenman that he favored shooting the Nazi leaders. Stalin thought they should be tried first, then shot afterwards.[8] In April 1945, when President Roosevelt died, Vice President Harry Truman took over. He told Judge Rosenman to gather Allied support for a trial of war criminals. Now that victory was in sight, postwar plans had to be made.

A Trial Is Arranged

Rosenman got the approval for a trial from British, French, and Soviet foreign ministers at San Francisco in May 1945, at the organizing conference of the United Nations. The four Allies agreed to set up an international military court after their representatives had met to plan the prosecution. On May 2, President Truman appointed Supreme Court Justice Robert H. Jackson to draft the basic rules for the trial and act as the chief prosecutor for the United States.

Jackson was an unusual choice. He was the last of the Justices to have "read law" with a mentor, rather than graduate from law school. He had only studied at law school for one year. For twenty years, Jackson developed a thriving practice and was active in the Democratic party.[9] When Franklin Roosevelt, governor of New York, became President in 1933, Jackson followed him to Washington. He held top offices in the Justice and Treasury departments before being named to the Supreme Court in 1941.

As President Truman's representative for the war crimes prosecution, Jackson traveled to Great Britain to meet with the British, French, and Soviet representatives. On June 26, 1945, a week after his arrival in London, formal negotiations began. They stretched over two months before a two-part accord was reached. The London Agreement expressed the mutual understanding of the four powers on how to set up an international court. Also, a charter spelled out legal rules for "the just and prompt trial and punishment of the major war criminals of the European Axis."[10]

Jackson later explained that most of the problems in connection with the prosecution were due to basic differences between the American-British and the French-Russian types of law. For example, an American judge acts as a referee between prosecutors and defense attorneys, who cross-examine witnesses. A French judge takes an active part in the questioning, with attorneys playing a lesser role.[11] There was also the Anglo-American concept of conspiracy, which made those who planned a crime together equally guilty. But that concept was not a part of Continental law.

Another problem was the differences between Western and Soviet representatives. Jackson wanted the trial to focus on the waging of "wars of aggression" by the Nazis. This aggression went against a number of treaties Germany had signed, notably the Kellogg-Briand Pact of August 1928, designed to "outlaw war." It was important to place responsibility on the Nazi leaders, Jackson argued, since

The chief prosecutor for the United States was Robert Jackson, on leave from the United States Supreme Court.

Americans "regarded Germany's resort to war as illegal from the outset, as an illegitimate attack on the international peace and order."[12]

Jackson's call for an international legal order clashed with views of the French and Soviet delegates at the London Conference. The French representative argued that to make aggression a crime would amount to overturning centuries of legal history. It would also be "ex post facto legislation," that is, punishing something that was legal before the law was adopted.[13] General I. T. Nikitchenko, vice president of the Soviet Supreme Court, was evidently concerned that German defendants might point the finger at the Soviet Union. After all, its attack on Finland in 1940 had been condemned as aggression by the League of Nations (predecessor of the United Nations). And the Soviets were still occupying Poland and the Baltic states—Lithuania, Latvia, and Estonia.[14]

Nikitchenko proposed an alternative to a general criminal charge against aggression. Namely, he favored limiting the charge to actions "by the European Axis in violation of international laws and treaties." But Jackson believed, "if certain acts in violation of treaties are crimes, they are crimes whether the United States does them or whether Germany does them."[15] Only on the last day of the conference was a compromise worked out. The crimes would be defined in general terms, but the jurisdiction (legal authority) of the court would be limited to trying war criminals "of the European Axis."[16]

Another difference between the American and Soviet

delegates had to do with the idea of conspiracy. If German military leaders, for example, had plotted together to launch an invasion of a neighboring country, then, according to Jackson, the General Staff could be indicted (formally charged with committing a crime) as a group. The same went for the Gestapo, the *SS* (the elite storm troopers), and other Nazi organizations. But Nikitchenko did not agree. At the Yalta conference, he said, Stalin, Roosevelt, and Churchill had already jointly condemned the SS and the Gestapo. How, he asked, could a court find any Nazi group innocent when it had already been found guilty by the Allied leaders at Yalta.[17]

Jackson replied that the opinions of government leaders could not take the place of proper courts. "The President of the United States has no power to convict anybody. . . . He can only accuse." Therefore, the wartime "declarations are an accusation and not a conviction. That requires a judicial finding." Without such a judgment based on evidence, the accused would simply be subject to "political executions . . . I have no sympathy with these [accused] men, but, if we are going to have a trial, then it must be an actual trial."[18]

This difference of opinion was resolved. The final indictment (formal charge) *did* include organizations as well as individuals. Unless the Western judges found the accused guilty "beyond a reasonable doubt," they would not convict them. The Soviet judges, on the other hand, saw the outcome of the trial as a foregone conclusion. "The fact that the Nazi leaders are criminals has already been established," Nikitchenko said. "The task of the Tribunal is only to determine the measure of guilt of each particular person and mete out [hand out] the necessary punishment—the sentences."[19]

The Charges Are Agreed To

Despite their differences, all four countries agreed on the following charges against the top Nazi leaders and organizations:

1) There were two "crimes against peace,"

- first, conspiring (planning) to seize power, establishing a criminal state, and preparing to wage wars of aggression; and

- second, the actual conduct of such wars;

2) Committing "war crimes," including murdering civilians or deporting them to slave labor, "murder or ill-treatment of prisoners of war," killing hostages, plunder, and "wanton destruction."

3) Crimes against humanity, such as "murder, extermination, enslavement, deportation and other inhuman acts committed against any civilian population" as well as "persecutions on political, racial or religious grounds."[20]

It had taken nearly three years for the Allies to agree on an international trial for Nazi war criminals. In the final months of World War II, there was a greater sense of urgency to get on with this task. American troops began to see evidence of "crimes against humanity" in camps like

American guards patrol the entrance to the Palace of Justice where the Nuremberg Trials took place.

Dachau. Soviet troops had been finding even more gruesome death camps in Poland, notably Auschwitz and Birkenau. Millions had been killed there. Freight trains full of Jews from Eastern Europe (Greece, Yugoslavia, Hungary, Poland and Romania, for example) kept bringing more victims to the death camps until the Nazi armies had been beaten back.

How would the Nazi leaders be caught? Some of them had died in battle or had committed suicide. Others fled from the advancing Soviet army, expecting to be treated more leniently by American and British troops. A few put on disguises and tried to slip through the front lines.

At the top of everybody's wanted list was Adolf Hitler, who had seized power in January 1933. The führer had personally taken charge of the war and made the killing of Jews his top priority. In his manifesto, *Mein Kampf* (My Struggle), Hitler had called Jews "the true enemy of our present-day world . . . the evil enemy of mankind, [and] the true cause of all suffering."[21] In 1939, Hitler told the *Reichstag* (the German lawmakers), that the Jewish race in Europe would be wiped out.[22]

Hitler had ordered the German invasion of neighboring countries, starting with the forced takeover of Austria in March 1938. He began World War II by having the security police dress concentration camp prisoners in Polish uniforms and murder them on the German border "to show that they had been killed while attacking."[23] The corpses were shown to the press and became an "excuse" for attacking

Poland on September 1, 1939. A series of attacks on other countries followed.

Hitler had shown no mercy toward his political enemies at home after he took control. And his armies imposed a brutal occupation on the countries they invaded.

Eventually, the Soviet Army pushed the German troops back in the crucial Battle of Stalingrad in November 1942. The British defeated German and Italian armies in North Africa. United States troops captured Sicily in 1943 and soon forced Italy out of the war. American, British, and French troops landed in Normandy, France, on D-day (June 6, 1944). Another ten months of bloody combat followed.

Finally, the Allies defeated the *Wehrmacht*, the German armed forces. Hitler and a handful of his lieutenants were surrounded in Berlin toward the end of April 1945. With Soviet troops closing in on him, Hitler told his followers to escape. After poisoning his dog, Blondi, Hitler killed himself and his wife, Eva Braun. Propaganda boss Goebbels followed Hitler by killing his wife and six children, then himself.

Hitler had claimed total responsibility for Germany's actions, whether it was the killing of Jews in concentration camps or the invasion of neighboring countries and making their people his slaves. His death now left a major problem for the Allies. How could they convict the members of Hitler's inner circle, all of whom would claim they were only following orders? In Article 8 of the international court's charter, the validity of such a defense was specifically ruled out. But even while legally denying it, the Allies could expect that nearly all of the Nazi leaders would blame their dead leader, Hitler.

Soon after Hitler's suicide, the Soviet army occupied the eastern part of Germany, including Berlin. American troops had taken the central and southern parts. The British forces ended up in the north. Each of these became a "zone of occupation." When it came time to decide where to hold a trial of major Nazi war criminals, the Americans suggested Nuremberg, a Bavarian city in the American zone. The Russians held out for Berlin, but they eventually agreed with the other Allies.

Nuremberg was an appropriate site because the biggest rallies in Hitler's time of triumph had been held there. It would be ironic as well to have the Nazis tried in Nuremberg, where they had marched in front of thousands of cheering supporters. Nuremberg was also where the Nuremberg Laws had stripped Jews of German citizenship in 1935. Most of the city had been destroyed in the fierce final battles and bombings of the war. On the outskirts of the city, however, was a Palace of Justice, which could be repaired quickly. Next to it was a prison that had enough room in its cellblock for the two dozen top-level Nazi leaders who were on trial.

chapter three

ASSEMBLING THE CAST FOR THE TRIAL

NAZI REGIME—The list of twenty-four accused Nazi leaders soon dwindled to twenty-two. Martin Bormann, the deputy führer who headed the Reich Security Office, could not be located but was tried in absentia (without actually being present). He was killed while trying to cross the Russian lines. It would take a long time before his body was found in the ruins of Berlin. Gustav Krupp von Bohlen, the seventy-eight-year-old head of the firm that supplied weapons to the Wehrmacht and used slave labor in its factories, was excused. His attorney pleaded that he was too senile to stand trial and, despite prosecutor objections, the court accepted the plea. (Krupp's son Alfried was eventually tried with eleven other executives of the firm in one of the dozen trials of "lesser war criminals" following the main trial at Nuremberg.)

That left twenty-two war criminals. Robert Ley, chief of the so-called Labor Front that had rounded up thousands of European workers for Germany, believed he had no chance of being found innocent. He managed to hang himself in his cell. In his suicide note, Ley asked himself why disaster had struck Germany. He answered, "We deserted God, and so God deserted us."[1]

One of the remaining twenty-one leaders charged with war crimes was Hans Fritzsche, the chief Nazi radio broadcaster. With his boss, propaganda chief Goebbels, dead, Fritzsche was asked to defend commentaries in which he had attacked Jews, prepared his countrymen for war, and urged Germans to fight for Hitler's regime to the death.[2] Fritzsche was not well known outside Germany.

But everyone knew about Hermann Goering, the head of the German air force. He was Hitler's chosen successor, but he fled Berlin. A World War I flying ace, Goering had shot down twenty-five enemy planes and earned two top military medals. In 1921, three years after the first war's end, Goering had joined Hitler's Nazi forces. He commanded the first storm troopers, then helped link up the Nazis to the highest-ranking officers in the army. After his election to the Reichstag in 1928, he was a key figure in the process of turning the government over to Hitler in 1933.

In occupied countries during World War II, Goering indulged his taste for art by sending freight cars of stolen works to his Prussian estate. When he was taken into American custody, he weighed 264 pounds (at five feet six inches) and had about forty thousand pills of synthetic morphine (a pain killer) in his sixteen pieces of matching luggage.[3] By then he had fallen from Hitler's favor and had fled from Berlin. The Führer was angry during his final days when he received Goering's message asking whether it was time he took over as head of state. One of Hitler's last commands was to order Goering's arrest as a traitor.

Colonel Burton C. Andrus, of the United States Army, had been in charge of the interrogation center in Luxembourg where Goering and other defendants were questioned. He was shocked to see the drugs in Goering's luggage. Andrus was determined to cut Goering back from his forty pills a day. Within two months, while Goering "whined and wailed," Colonel Andrus had him "completely free of the drug habit."[4] Without the drugs, Goering's health improved and his weight decreased. Prison searches also led to the confiscation of potassium cyanide pills Goering had hidden in his clothing and in a can of instant coffee. (It was later discovered, however, that Goering hid one suicide pill on his body.)

Key prisoners like Goering were taken and questioned by United States intelligence agents of the Office of Strategic Services (OSS), predecessor of the Central Intelligence Agency (CIA). The OSS was commanded by General William J. ("Wild Bill") Donovan. Donovan had been the most decorated officer from the United States during World War I, and a partner in a leading law firm after the war. At first, Jackson relied on the crucial help of OSS agents in preparing background files on the future defendants. But soon differences between Jackson and Donovan developed.

Donovan envisioned a trial in which some of the top Nazis would testify against each other. Herman Goering, for example, made no secret of his dislike of ex-foreign minister

Colonel Burton C. Andrus, of the United States Army, was in charge of the interrogation center in Luxembourg where Hermann Goering and other defendants were questioned. Under Andrus's watchful eye, Goering overcame his morphine addiction.

Joachim von Ribbentrop, national bank president Hjalmar Schacht, slave labor recruiter Fritz Sauckel, or Hitler's personal architect, Albert Speer. Donovan spent ten days questioning Goering. He wore a uniform with even more medals than Goering's.[5] Goering seemed ready to testify against his old rivals if he were guaranteed a soldier's death by firing squad instead of a shameful hanging.[6] Speer sent memos to Jackson offering to share some of his military secrets in return for special favors. Schacht approached Donovan with inside information of his own, also angling for a deal.[7]

Jackson decided that it would be wrong to rely on some of the defendants turning state's evidence (testifying for the prosecution), since "it always gives the conviction a bad odor. We decided it would be better to lose our case against some defendants than to win by a deal that would discredit the judgment."[8] As he was preparing for the trial, Jackson was aware that mountains of incriminating documents had been captured.

Hans Frank, the wartime governor of Poland, was found with a forty-volume set of his diaries. An OSS team had discovered ten tons of damaging Nazi records behind the bricked wall of a dungeon in Bavaria.[9] There were also detailed records from the death camps in Poland. There were even films showing the burning down of the Warsaw ghetto and the death of its last Jewish residents. Even though Donovan felt this evidence was not as powerful as live testimony, Jackson decided to make it the basis of his case. Therefore, before the trial began, Donovan's job was over.

But before his departure, Donovan made a case for a quick trial conducted under German law. He thought that if accusations came directly from some of the accused, the German people would accept the outcome as fair—that they and the world would share a view of Nazi crimes as an "unprecedented outrage against humanity."[10] He also argued against charging the German general staff and other groups with collective crimes. On both points, Jackson overruled him.

Donovan tried to discredit the defense of Rudolf Hess. When he was Hitler's deputy, Hess had flown to Scotland in May 1941 on a private mission to bring Germany's war with England to an end. After he parachuted, Hess was taken prisoner. British doctors said he was mentally ill, and was suffering from periods of amnesia (loss of memory). Now back in Germany for his trial, Allied doctors said that he did have amnesia but was not legally insane, so would have to stand trial. Donovan watched Hess closely while showing him films where he had appeared at rallies alongside Hitler. But Hess showed no emotion and continued to insist he could not remember that part of his life. He refused to meet with his lawyer or to take any part in the forthcoming trial.[11]

Donovan's legal papers are now available in the archives of Cornell Law School. They reveal little beyond what is already known. His main role seems to have been to gather the documents that Jackson's staff needed for the prosecution. Only rarely was Donovan's advice important. For example, when the seating of the defendants was being discussed, the initial plan was to seat them on benches.

Donovan pointed out, however, that it would not look good if some of the older men grew so tired that they toppled off a bench. Instead, the accused sat in seats with backs.[12]

One of those old men was Hjalmar Horace Greeley Schacht. He had been given his middle names for the American abolitionist (antislavery activist). Schacht's family had lived in the United States for six years in the 1870s before returning to Germany. Schacht had studied medicine and political science before getting a doctorate in economics. He had a distinguished career in banking.

As president of the *Reichsbank* (the German central bank) in 1923, Schacht got a British loan to stop Germany's record inflation. He supported Hitler's cause because the Nazis promised an end to strikes. He persuaded industrialists (factory owners) to support Hitler. Later, in his defense, he would argue that he only wanted to do what was good for business.[13] As economics minister, Schacht spoke in favor of the Nazi program. Yet he was opposed to Goering's program to re-arm Germany. He also was against killing Jews, yet he supported pushing them out of the German economy and seizing their property.[14] "The Jews must realize that their influence in Germany has disappeared for all time," he said in a 1935 speech.[15]

As Hitler prepared for war, Schacht became privately critical but kept praising Hitler publicly. As a result of his cautious conversations with a group that plotted to assassinate the Führer on July 20, 1944, Schacht was arrested. When the Americans picked him to be tried at Nuremberg, Schacht had already been a prisoner at three concentration

Hitler's chosen successor was Hermann Goering, one of the more recognizable figures at the Nuremberg Trials.

camps, including Dachau. He acted as if it were incredible that he could now be accused of war crimes. Would his second thoughts about Hitler get him off the hook? Or would his earlier promotion of the Nazi cause lead to a guilty verdict?

General Donovan had expressed doubts about punishing German military leaders as war criminals. Two of the generals who were brought to trial at Nuremberg had done more than their soldierly duty to the Nazi regime. Wilhelm Keitel and Alfred Jodl (pronounced yodel) stood accused of being accomplices of the special forces that committed mass murder of Jews in Poland and the Soviet Union. Keitel had also been head of the Wehrmacht supreme command for five years. He passed on Hitler's orders. That meant disregarding the Geneva Conventions—the international treaties that, since 1846, had regulated the treatment of prisoners and civilians during wartime.

In December 1942, for example, Keitel had issued an order to treat with no mercy any resistance fighters on the Russian front. The Geneva Convention provision calling for prisoners to be treated humanely was not to apply, he wrote. Instead he called for "the greatest brutality against the bands both in the East and in the Balkans."[16] He concluded, "The troops are therefore empowered and, in duty, bound to use without mitigation [restraint] even against women and children any means that will lead to success." In other words, no one from an enemy country would be allowed to stand in the way of German victory.

Other orders from the Führer that were relayed by Keitel

included the so-called "Commissar Order." After the German invasion of Russia on June 22, 1941, any political officers of the Soviet army as well as Allied soldiers on sabotage missions, were to be shot.[17] Another order directed German troops to burn down any village in which resistance fighters were found. Fifty to one hundred hostages were to be killed for the murder of a single German soldier. Keitel also signed a so-called "Night and Fog" decree on December 7, 1941, which ordered all people suspected of resisting the German occupation to be shipped to concentration camps.

Below Keitel's rank of field marshal was his fellow defendant, Colonel General Jodl, a Bavarian officer who had been wounded in World War I. Under Hitler, Jodl became chief of the High Command operations staff. Through victories, then defeats, Jodl kept his faith in Hitler as a military genius. In November 1943, he told the Nazi governors that "our trust and faith in the Führer is boundless. . . . A Europe under the whip of American Jews or Bolshevik commissars is unthinkable."[18]

Jodl had disagreed at times with Hitler on some specific strategies, but he maintained his loyalty to the Nazi system until the end. He was convinced that he was not a war criminal—merely a soldier who obeyed orders from the head of state.[19] Lieutenant Colonel William Dunn, the United States army psychiatrist, wrote that Jodl said "that he had conducted himself as a soldier should in carrying out the duties to his country and government." Dunn observed that Jodl "has no inner discomfort about the war but is apparently considerably disturbed about the evidence of the atrocities."[20] This matched Keitel's comments, that "the responsibilities of a soldier [were] to accept orders and to obey."[21]

Whatever their scruples may have been, Keitel and Jodl had supported measures that broke the rules for warfare set up by the Geneva Conventions. For example, in May 1941, they had joined in an order to shoot without trial those "enemy civilians" who were guilty of offenses against German troops.[22] Keitel and Jodl also signed another order to execute any captured commandos, as well as to recruit forced labor in Denmark, Holland, France, and Belgium.[23] Finally, there was the already mentioned "Commissar Order," which permitted the execution of political officers in the Soviet Army.

The Nazi generals argued that they had only been good soldiers. But the basic guidelines for the trial prevented them from using this as a defense. If they followed Hitler's orders by passing along his illegal orders, they would now have to take personal responsibility. Only after they had been convicted could they use Hitler's orders as a way to reduce their sentences.

In the meantime, they had a month to select a lawyer. The staff of the international tribunal would then try to locate the one they selected. Or they could have a defender appointed for them by the court. As it turned out, practically all the defense lawyers were happy to take on their assignments at Nuremberg. In the postwar chaos of Germany in

1945, this assignment at least assured attorneys of work, decent housing, and food.

When Goering picked Otto Stahmer to be his lawyer, some of the tribunal staff questioned whether they should accept someone known to be a staunch Nazi. Justice Jackson, however, said that the trial guidelines were clear on this point: the choice of counsel was to be entirely free. There was no way to disqualify someone for his Nazi sympathies.

Defendants like Goering would later complain that they were facing a "court of the victors," those who had defeated them in World War II. They would also argue that they had too little time to prepare their defense. They further complained about the rule that they could apply for any court document to be used in their defense only if it were first released from the prosecutors' files. But they could not claim that they were denied attorneys of their choice or that they could not get their defense arguments into the court's records.

chapter four

SETTING THE STAGE FOR THE TRIAL

NAZIS ON TRIAL—The twenty-one defendants who were waiting for the Nuremberg trial to start in November 1945 were a mixed group. Some of them, like Hermann Goering and Rudolf Hess, had been in the inner circle around Hitler from the earliest days. Others, like Wilhelm Keitel and Alfred Jodl, both generals, had been used by Hitler to make sure that his most extreme military orders were followed carefully. The two naval commanders, Erich Raeder and Karl Doenitz, seemed to have less direct involvement in war crimes. However, the two admirals were accused of waging total submarine warfare, or trying to sink not only warships but also commercial ships.

There were brutal governors of countries occupied by the Nazis, such as Hans Frank in Poland and Arthur Seyss-Inquart in the Netherlands. Then there were the economic bosses, such as Fritz Sauckel, who had rounded up slave laborers, and Albert Speer, who was ready to use slave labor in the factories he ran. Foreign Minister Joachim von Ribbentrop was accused of conducting a foreign policy that lured neighboring governments into a false belief that Hitler would respect their independence, and then invading them anyway. Constantin von Neurath had also been a foreign minister, but his main service to Hitler had been in the early 1930s. Then he had supported German occupation of the Rhineland—an area that had been taken away from Germany as punishment after World War I.

Some defendants seemed to be primarily stand-ins for their notorious bosses, who had died. For example, in place of propaganda chief Goebbels was his assistant Hans Fritzsche. The head of the Reich security office, Ernst Kaltenbrunner, filled in for his boss, Gestapo chief Heinrich Himmler.

Others, like former chancellor Franz von Papen, Interior Minister Wilhelm Frick, and bank president Hjalmar Schacht, were career politicians, who had paved the way for Hitler's takeover in 1933. They had lost a lot of their influence in later years. A much more important figure had been Baldur von Schirach, head of the Hitler Youth, who had brainwashed a generation of German children into becoming "good soldiers" for Hitler. Julius Streicher had been in charge of spreading hatred of the Jews through his writings. And Alfred Rosenberg had written a shelf of books spelling out Nazi ideology. His war crime, however, consisted of running the office for "Eastern occupied territories." That meant that, in name, if not always in fact, he had supervised horrible crimes in Russia and Poland.

A Variety of Charges

The charges against some of the accused seemed more serious than others. The ringleaders were the men who had carried out Hitler's orders and been directly in charge of the death camps and torture chambers. The army generals commanded troops that routinely butchered civilians. The navy admirals, however, could only be accused of sinking nonmilitary ships. Some defendants faced more charges than others, such as conspiracy, waging aggressive war, committing war crimes, and committing crimes against humanity.

Organizations Charged

Along with the individual men who would appear in court, there were also six Nazi organizations being accused. If those groups were convicted, any of their individual members could then be found guilty of a crime, unless they could prove they had been forced to participate. Yet these six groups also differed in the degree to which they had been involved in war crimes.

There was little doubt about the violence used by the feared Gestapo, the SS and SD, the security police, and the leadership corps of the Nazi party. But cases against three other organizations seemed to be less certain. The SA, for example, had seen its storm troopers fade as an effective force after the early days of the regime. The *Reichskabinett* (national cabinet), made up of ministers of the Nazi government, had stopped having regular meetings after 1937. And the general staff and high command had lost their authority as war approached and Hitler took personal command of the armed forces.

For prosecutor Jackson, the individual defendants and the organizations were all part of one giant conspiracy—so that those who had only been in charge of office clerks were as guilty as the commanders of regiments. They all pleaded innocent to all charges. But their protests that they had not

Dr. Otto Stahmer, a judge from Kiel (at front right), presents the defense for Hermann Goering. Some members of the tribunal staff did not want Stahmer, a staunch Nazi, to represent Goering.

known the extent of the war crimes could not possibly be true. Their signatures on the execution orders contradicted their testimony.

Getting Ready for a Trial

Before the defendants could take the stand, the courtroom had to be made ready for this remarkable trial. Two hundred fifty reporters would flock to Nuremberg. Four judges, flanked by alternates, would listen to the proceedings in English, German, French, and Russian. The defendants and their lawyers had to be able to respond to questions in these four languages. Today we are used to hearing so-called simultaneous translation, which is used at the United Nations. But in 1945, nothing on this scale had ever been attempted.

Specially trained interpreters in the auditorium spoke into four separate microphones. With only a slight delay, the words of a woman speaking in English were translated into French, German and Russian. The words could be heard through headsets, while a dial allowed listeners to switch from one language to another.[1] For the system to work at Nuremberg, interpreters had to be trained to start translating within eight seconds, so that they would not lose the meaning of the testimony. It was not always easy, especially with very long German sentences.

Before the communications system could be set up, however, the site of the trial had to be put back into usable shape. The Palace of Justice had been heavily damaged during the last stand of the Nazi troops in the area. It would take hundreds of German prisoners of war to restore the building.[2]

The project was directed by Captain Dan Kiley of the OSS, an architect who had run a firm in Washington that built wartime housing. Now he was in charge of breaking down walls to double the courtroom's seating. The attic would be converted into a visitors' gallery. He also got rid of the ornate chandeliers and put in fluorescent lighting. Then he needed to find office space for about six hundred staff members.[3] Some nearby factories supplied building materials, while glass had to be flown in from Belgium. Office furniture was made to order.

Rumors had been circulating that secret Nazi groups would try to free the Nazi prisoners who were on trial. So the building had to be separated from the rest of the city. The entire complex of five buildings was surrounded by barbed wire. It was then guarded by American tanks, artillery, anti-aircraft guns, infantry, and military police.

Another concern was the prevention of further suicides by the defendants before the trial started. Robert Ley had hanged himself from a water pipe with a strip of toweling. The iron bars on the windows of the cells were removed and the openings covered with hard plastic. The prisoners had to surrender their ties and shoelaces, although they would be returned before they appeared in court. They all had to sleep with their hands outside the covers. And a military police officer watched each cell around the clock. The only area of privacy was the toilet, which was not visible from the peephole in the cell door.[4]

There was also a new assignment for Gustav M. Gilbert, an army officer who spoke fluent German. He had been in army intelligence, questioning German prisoners. Then he had come to Nuremberg to serve as an interpreter for the prison psychiatrist, Major Douglas Kelley. Now Colonel Andrus, the prison warden, persuaded Gilbert to use his professional training as a psychologist by closely watching the defendants. He would stay with them at meals and even observe them in the shower.

Gilbert spoke with each of the prisoners. After these talks, he recorded his notes. These notes would make up a future book. One of his first projects was to ask each defendant to write what he thought of the charges against him.

In the margins of the official papers, Goering expressed his hatred for this trial. He wrote, "The victor will always be the judge, and the [defeated] the accused."[5] Former interior minister Frick echoed that opinion. He said, "The whole indictment rests on the assumption of a fictitious conspiracy."[6] The anti-Semitic (anti-Jewish) Streicher was true to form when he wrote, "This trial is a triumph of World Jewry!"[7]

The military officers saw themselves as merely following Hitler's commands. Keitel said, "For a soldier, orders are orders." Jodl only rejected the form of the charges, not the charges themselves. He said, "I regret the mixture of justified accusations and political propaganda."[8] Admiral Doenitz shrugged the whole thing off saying, "None of these indictment counts concern me in the least—typical American humor."

A handful of the defendants showed remorse. Frank, the

former governor of Poland, wrote, "I regard this trial as a God-willed court, destined to examine and put to an end the terrible [era of] suffering under Adolf Hitler."[9] Hitler Youth leader Baldur von Schirach expressed his regret over the anti-Jewish campaign, saying, "The whole misfortune comes from racial politics."[10] Weapons minister Speer also accepted the need for a trial, but he stopped short of accepting any personal responsibility. He said, "The trial is necessary. There is a common responsibility for such horrible crimes even in an authoritarian system."[11]

Propagandist Hans Fritzsche, for one, did not try to minimize the charges. He wrote, "It is the most terrible

In an official German photo, the burning of the Warsaw ghetto can be seen, as survivors are marched off to a square for transfer to the death camp.

indictment of all times. Only one thing is more terrible—the indictment of the German people."[12] Hitler's deputy, Rudolf Hess, insisted on his amnesia as a defense, writing in English, "I can't remember." But labor boss Fritz Sauckel understood the consequences of his actions. He said, "The abyss between the ideal of a social community, which I imagined and [supported] as a former seaman and worker, and the terrible happenings in the concentration camps, has shaken me deeply."[13]

The diplomat Franz von Papen composed the longest comment, which took up the common theme of blaming all the evil on Hitler. He said that German leaders had been irresponsible in starting the war. He could not understand how his people had committed so many crimes. But he suspected that idol worship and Hitler's unrelenting rule were at fault. Hitler had become a pathological liar over the years.[14]

Banker Hjalmar Schacht conveniently forgot that he helped to put the Nazis into power, saying, "I do not understand at all why I have been accused."[15] No one was sure whether Hess had really lost his memory. Was it also possible that Schacht was playing dumb?

Spiritual Guidance Offered

Before the start of the trial, the defendants were also offered the choice of two United States Army chaplains to be their spiritual counselors. These counselors were provided for prisoners of war, according to the rules of the Geneva Convention. Father Sixtus O'Connor, from Oxford, New

York, offered services to the six Catholic prisoners. Major Henry F. Gerecke, from St. Louis, Missouri, counseled the fifteen Protestants.

Father O'Connor had learned German before the war as a student at the University of Munich. Now he seemed to have one notable success, as Hans Frank asked to be rebaptized.[16] Psychologist Gilbert was at first skeptical about Frank's sincerity, but he eventually felt Frank (along with von Schirach) was showing real remorse.[17] Goering hollered at Frank for having turned his complete set of wartime diaries over to the Americans. Frank claimed to have done so out of religious conviction, but it is possible he thought the diaries would help lessen his guilt, and thus the severity of his punishment.

It may seem odd that the men accused of war crimes in Nuremberg turned to religion. The Nazis had used their ideology to fight established Christian churches. But these defendants were now facing possible death sentences. They were returning to the faith of their childhood. Also, the chaplains were two of the only officials they met who did not judge them. But they were not all sincere. For example, Goering told the prison psychologist, "Prayers, hell! It's just a chance to get out of this damn cell for a half hour."[18]

There was barely one month between the serving of the indictments and the scheduled start of the trial on November 20, 1945. The French and Russian prosecutors asked to have more time to prepare the case. The Americans insisted on proceeding quickly, however, before the impact on the world was lost.[19] The judges met briefly to consider pretrial motions of the defense attorneys who asked that the trial be stopped. The trial would be illegal, they claimed, because it was biased and used ex post facto accusations—that is, it cited some acts that had not been crimes at the time they were committed. The judges took two days to reject this argument, although they said that the defendants would have a chance to raise this point again later.[20]

Trial Set to Begin

The stage was now set for the opening of the Nuremberg trial. The American staff was equal in numbers to the combined British, French, and Russian staffers. The Americans had the decisive voice in framing the indictment, scheduling the trial, and setting the rules. Now they would take the lead in the prosecution.

Robert Jackson was going to present the first charge, conspiracy in seizing power and in waging war. He would be followed by Sir Hartley Shawcross, the British chief prosecutor, who would cover the second charge, the actual crimes against peace. Then Francois de Menthon, the chief prosecutor for France, would cover part of two other charges, war crimes and crimes against humanity. R. A. Rudenko, the Soviet chief prosecutor, was going to conclude by presenting evidence of war crimes and crimes against humanity in eastern Europe.[21]

This unique international trial for war crimes was about to begin.

chapter five

THE CASE FOR THE PROSECUTION

THE TRIAL—At 11:00 A.M. on November 20, 1945, Lord Justice Geoffrey Lawrence opened the Nuremberg proceedings. He had been selected by his colleagues as presiding judge because of his experience as Lord Chief Justice of England. The Russians, at first, wanted the presidency of the court to be shared among the four judges, but they eventually agreed that Lawrence was the best choice. He was a well-known judge and had a reputation for fairness, even among the Germans.

"This trial is unique in the history of jurisprudence [science of law] of the world and of supreme importance to millions of people all over the globe," the British judge began.[1] Next to Lawrence at the front of the courtroom were seven other judges. France, Britain, the United States, and the Soviet Union had each named a judge and an alternate. Law professor Donnedieu de Vabres was the French judge, former Attorney General Francis Biddle the American one, and Major General Iona T. Nikitchenko the Soviet one.

Formal Charges Read

The entire first day was spent reading the indictment (formal charges) against the defendants. The first charge dealt with conspiracy, both in the Nazi seizure of power and the planning of war. The second charge—crimes against peace—consisted mainly of listing the countries German troops had invaded. The third charge—war crimes—was a catalog of horrible crimes in each of the Nazi-occupied countries. It included the mistreatment of prisoners, the killing of hostages, the use of forced and slave labor, and the plunder and destruction of property. "Crimes against humanity" was the fourth charge, directed at the torture of civilians in concentration camps and the mass killing of Jews, known as genocide, or the deliberate killing of an entire people.[2]

Additional Charges

There were also three additions to the indictment. Appendix A specified the charges against each of the defendants. Appendix B did the same for the six Nazi organizations. Appendix C listed twenty-six international treaties that had been violated by the Nazis.

This formal legal presentation did not electrify the courtroom in Nuremberg. The real drama began on the second day with Robert Jackson's opening speech for the prosecution. He pointed to the "twenty-odd broken men" in the prisoners' dock. "Merely as individuals, their fate is of little consequence to the world," he said. "What makes this inquest significant is that these prisoners represent sinister influences that will lurk in the world long after their bodies have returned to dust. They are living symbols of racial hatreds, of terrorism and violence, of the arrogance and cruelty of power."[3]

Jackson went on to say that the Allies would not simply punish the prisoners who had been their enemies. Instead, they would give them a fair trial that would stand up later to the judgment of history. But, only eight months after the war ended, there were no local courts available, only an international court of the victorious Allies.[4]

Was there any other choice? No, said Jackson. "Did we spend American lives to capture them only to save them from punishment?" The prisoners could not simply be released. And there were no neutral countries available for an unbiased trial. But the Allies could make sure that their enemies received a fair trial. They would be given "a fair opportunity to defend themselves—a favor which these men, when in power, rarely extended to their fellow countrymen."[5] The Nazis had hanged their enemies after torturing some of them to confess in court. Here, the accused would be presumed innocent.

A guilty verdict would depend on the ability of prosecutors to prove that criminal acts had been committed and that these defendants were responsible. Jackson said there would be no point in trying "to incriminate the whole German people."[6] If all the people had accepted the rule of the Nazis, they would not have had to be forced into submission from the outset by storm troopers and concentration camps. A key to the prosecution would be proving the case with thousands

Sir Hartley Shawcross, presenting the prosecution case for Great Britain. He argued the charge of crimes against peace.

of documents. The defendants had shown a "passion for thoroughness in putting things on paper." They also filmed their actions and "we will show you their own films."[7]

For example, said Jackson, records proved that about 60 percent of the Jews in Nazi-controlled Europe had been killed. That meant of 9,600,000, some 5,700,000 were missing and presumed dead.[8] Jackson went on to quote from Hans Frank, the Nazi ruler of Poland, who said, "The Jews are a race which has to be eliminated; whenever we catch one, it is his end."[9] Frank had also written, "Of course, I cannot eliminate all lice and Jews in only a year's time."[10]

Then Jackson read from a German general's report, "The Jewish Ghetto in Warsaw No Longer Exists." SS General Juergen Stroop told of troops using flames to demolish every last building where someone might be hiding. The last survivors jumped to their deaths or were gunned down in doorways.[11] They had managed to hold out with a few weapons against tanks and planes for twenty-eight days.

The rest of Jackson's speech was devoted to other Nazi crimes. He focused on the secret planning that preceded attacks on Czechoslovakia, Poland, and Russia.[12] Then came secret orders to "slaughter to the last man" any captured commandos or enemy flyers.[13] Finally, he described the forced shipment of five million slave laborers to Germany. They included young Russians, ages ten to fourteen, so that—as Rosenberg put it—there would be "a desired weakening of the biological force of the conquered people."[14]

What about the lack of precedent (related past cases)

that was required for a criminal case in domestic courts? Jackson said he was "not disturbed by the lack of judicial precedent."[15] The charter of this tribunal was an advance in international law. Besides, the war crimes and crimes against humanity that it spelled out were already "too familiar to need comment." The "crime against peace" posed a special problem. The charter's "weakness," Jackson admitted, was that it had not defined "aggression."[16] (This was a criticism of the Soviets who had resisted a broad definition, since it might be used against their own attacks on Poland and the Baltic states.) However, Jackson went on to offer his own summary of what defined an aggressor. In general, it applied to a state that attacked another state "with or without a declaration of war." Thus, the only military action that was legal would be acts "of legitimate self-defense."[17] The excuses Germany offered—for example, that it had gone to war to gain living space for its people—did not stand up.

Jackson's opening speech had taken almost the entire day. It had a dramatic effect on the newspaper reporters as reflected in the front-page stories that they filed. The relaxed defendants were suddenly alert in the overheated courtroom. Their earphones were glued to their heads as they listened to Jackson read from German documents describing in graphic detail the war crimes with which they were charged.[18] But the speech also unsettled the other three teams of prosecutors. Jackson seemed to stretch the broadly drawn conspiracy charge to include waging aggressive war, committing war crimes, and committing crimes against humanity, the areas left to the British, French, and Soviet prosecutors.

In a memo Jackson had written before the trial, he told an associate that the United States' team had to frame its charges "as a basis for keeping the bulk of the case in American hands." The other prosecutors would be left only the charges on specific acts in their area. Jackson would take "primary responsibility for the development of this case in all its aspects on the question of a common plan. . . ."[19]

As he showed in his opening speech, Jackson used the charge of conspiracy to go beyond the mere planning of Nazi crimes. He went on to list acts of aggression and then to describe how they led to actual atrocities. He and the assistant prosecutors for the United States introduced many key documents. By the court's rules, the same evidence could not be reintroduced by the three other sets of prosecutors.

Film Shows Images of Horror

Perhaps the most powerful impression during the American presentation was a film showing what the concentration camps looked like. There were graphic scenes of mounds of dead bodies. The liberating troops had filmed close-ups of the corpses, all skin and bones. Former camp guards were shown assisting in mass burials. Afterward, the defendants sat in stunned silence. Back in their cells, Hans Fritzsche said through his tears, "No power in heaven or earth will erase this shame from my country—not in generations—not in centuries!"[20] Goering complained, "Everyone was laughing with me [when he had described his part in the invasion of Austria earlier] and then they showed that awful film, and it just spoiled everything."[21] Frank told the prison psychologist Gilbert, "Don't let everyone tell you that they had no idea. Everyone sensed there was something horribly wrong . . . even if we did not know all the details. They didn't want to know."[22]

Soviet prosecutor R.A. Rudenko makes his case. He presented evidence of war crimes and crimes against humanity. Other prosecutors are seated behind him.

Documents Outline War Crimes

Some of the American assistant prosecutors now presented hundreds of documents to prove the charge of crimes against humanity. They presented evidence that nearly five million people from the conquered lands had been forced to work for Germany. Perhaps the worst treatment had been reserved for Russians and Poles. Martin Bormann, next to Hitler the highest Nazi party leader (who was being tried without actually being present), had announced,

> The Slavs are to work for us. Insofar as we don't need them, they may die. They should not receive the benefits of the German public health system. . . . As to food, they will not get any more than is absolutely necessary. We are masters; we come first.[23]

Frank, the governor of Poland, had enforced Hitler's orders in October 1939 that called for

> utilizing the country by means of ruthless exploitation; removal of all supplies—raw materials, machines, factory installations . . . reduction of the entire Polish economy to the absolute minimum necessary for the bare existence of the population. . . . Poland shall be treated as a colony; the Poles shall be the slaves of the Greater German World Empire.[24]

Thousands of Poles were deported from their homes and German colonists were brought in. Frank told his staff in January 1943,

> We must not be squeamish when we learn that a total of 17,000 people have been shot. After all, these people who were shot are also war victims. . . . We must remember that all of us who are gathered together here figure on Mr.

Roosevelt's list of war criminals. I have the honor of being Number One.[25]

The worst fate befell the Jews. In December 1941, Frank had estimated that Poland had a population of 2,500,000 Jews.[26] Just over one year later, in January 1943, he wrote in his diary, "At the present time we still have in [Poland] perhaps 100,000 Jews."[27] That meant that only four of every hundred still survived, and most of them were being worked to death in factories near prison camps. At the Nuremberg trial, one witness had been a close colleague of Adolf Eichmann, the Gestapo chief in charge of shipping Jews from all over Europe to the camps where they were killed. This witness was asked what Eichmann had told him about this program. He said,

> Eichmann personally always talked about at least four million Jews [killed]. Sometimes he even mentioned five million. . . . He said he would leap laughing into the grave because the feeling that he had five million people on his conscience would be for him a source of extraordinary satisfaction.[28]

Another prosecution witness had been an SS-man—part of the special "Death's Head" group of volunteers who guarded the camps. He testified that at the Mauthausen camp in Austria, prisoners were worked to death carrying heavy blocks of stone from a quarry. When they became too weak, they were "parachuted," that is, dropped from a hundred-foot-high cliff to their death. Others, including prisoners of war, had been shot in the neck while their height was supposedly being measured. Still others were sent to a gas chamber. These forms of execution were demonstrated to the Gestapo chief Kaltenbrunner. He denied that he had even visited Mauthausen, let alone witnessed any executions.[29] Yet documents showed that on April 27, 1945, a few days before the war ended, Kaltenbrunner had told the camp commandant that "at least a thousand inmates still have to die at Mauthausen each day."[30]

In this, as in most instances, the documents proved stronger than testimony from witnesses. But the mountain of papers had, at times, overwhelmed the American prosecutors. They occasionally failed to specify the connection of the papers to the defendants on trial. And they did not focus on their assignment—the conspiracy charge.[31] The weakest presentations had been during the case against Nazi groups, including the Leadership Corps, the cabinet, and the SA. The judge kept asking for the relevance of the stack of papers being introduced into evidence. Prosecutor Robert Storey said it was only meant to have a cumulative effect. The judges said such repetitive material had to be omitted.[32]

Because it took a while for the United States to make its case, it was clear that this would not be the quick trial that was expected. Three more sets of prosecutors were waiting to have their turn. It looked at the time as if another six months would be needed: Instead, the trial lasted a full year.

The British Case

On December 4, Sir Hartley Shawcross opened the British case. It focused on crimes against peace. The British could not argue about the German invasion of Czechoslovakia, since their prime minister, Neville Chamberlain, had given in to Hitler at the Munich conference of September 1938. But they could begin with the 1939 attack on Poland.

First, Shawcross disposed of two arguments that were sure to be central to the defense. Crimes against peace would be seen as ex post facto, that is, not covered by existing law when they occurred. "Can it really be said on behalf of these defendants," he asked,

Shown here are the judges at the Nuremberg Trials (left to right): Britain's Sir Norman Birkett and Sir Geoffrey Lawrence; the Soviet Union's Iona T. Nikitchenko and Alexander F. Volchkov; the United States's John J. Parker and Francis Biddle; France's Robert Falco and Henri Donnedieu de Vabres.

that the offense of these aggressive wars, which plunged
millions of people to their death, which . . . brought about
the torture and extermination of countless thousands of
innocent civilians, which devastated cities . . ., which has
brought the world to the brink of ruin from which it will take
generations to recover—will it be seriously said by these
defendants that such a war is only an offense, only an ille-
gality . . . but not a crime justiciable by any Tribunal?[33]

In other words, it would be unthinkable to allow the
defendants to avoid a trial for mass murder when a single
murder could be tried anywhere.

Next, Shawcross put to rest the defense that it was all
Hitler's fault and the accused had been merely following his
orders. He argued of Hitler's followers, "They are the men
whose support had built Hitler up into the position of power
he occupied; . . . whose initiative and planning often
conceived and certainly made possible the acts of aggression
done in Hitler's name."[34] How could one let the leaders off
for having done Hitler's bidding, when even a "common
soldier . . . is not called upon to obey illegal orders."[35]

A British assistant prosecutor then presented a record of
Hitler's meeting with his generals in May 1939. He ordered
them to prepare for an attack on Poland, even though it
might lead to general war. The attack required that "western
powers keep out of it. If this is impossible, then it will be
better to attack in the West and to settle with Poland at the
same time." First, Hitler said, "Dutch and Belgian air bases
must be occupied by armed force. Declarations of neutrality
must be ignored."[36] If England did back Poland, "we must
occupy Holland with lightning speed. . . . The occupation of

Holland and Belgium and the defeat of France will establish fundamental conditions for the successful war against England." Hitler was sure that "Russia will show herself to be disinterested in the destruction of Poland."[37]

On August 22, 1939, just nine days before Hitler ordered the attack on Poland, he had a final meeting with his commanders. He had sent Joachim von Ribbentrop to Moscow to negotiate a secret treaty dividing Poland between Germany and Russia. He told the generals that Poland, once conquered, would supply them with

> grain, cattle, coal, lead and zinc. . . . I am only afraid that at the last minute some *Schweinehund* [dirty dog] will make a proposal for mediation. . . . Our economic situation is such . . . that we cannot hold out more than a few years. Goering can confirm this. We have no other choice; we must act.[38]

Hermann Goering, as the highest-ranking officer, jumped up to pledge the Wehrmacht's support to Hitler.[39]

The British case had brought back a sharp focus to the trial. The prosecutors had pointed to treaties of friendship that became part of international law when they were signed by Germany. Then they had linked the military and diplomatic defendants to the breach of these treaties, as country after country had been attacked. None of them had dared to speak out against Hitler's commands.

The French Case

On January 17, 1946, Francois de Menthon opened the French case about crimes against humanity. He was not only a law professor, but had also been active in the anti-Nazi underground after he escaped from a German prison. His speech was a clear summary of existing international law that covered the racist crimes of the defendants. He said:

> France, who was systematically plundered and ruined; France, so many of whose sons were tortured and murdered in the jails of the Gestapo or in their concentration camps; France asks you . . . in the names of the heroic martyrs of the Resistance . . . that justice be done.[40]

De Menthon argued that the vast pattern of crimes could be seen as an attempt by the Nazis to abandon civilized values and turn people "back into barbarism." The moving force was racism that granted only so-called Aryans the right to live. He quoted the defendant, Rosenberg, as denying that souls belong to "the Church of God." The defendant

The two American members of the tribunal were John J. Parker (left) and senior Judge Francis Biddle (right).

said instead that everyone's body and soul belong "to the Germanic state."[41]

This opening address was followed by documents and witnesses presented by assistant prosecutors. For the next six weeks, they detailed the Nazi takeover of occupied countries, the killing of hostages, the starvation and forced labor of the conquered people, and the horrors that awaited them in concentration camps.

Not only were these camps the scene of mass killing; they were also used for so-called medical experiments. Doctors had a seemingly unlimited supply of human subjects. Yet their sadistic research produced not a single significant new finding. For example, Dr. Sigmund Rascher, an air force physician, claimed he could use prisoners at Dachau to develop ways to rescue German fliers who bailed out in icy seas. If the inmates were immersed in freezing water long enough, they died. So they were frozen for only a short time and were quickly rewarmed. A prisoner who had worked at the "experimental station" said, "The victims came out looking like lobsters. Some lived but most of them died."[42]

Other inmates were tested for blood clotting after severe injuries were inflicted on them as a way of simulating battlefield conditions. Again, predictably, most of the men died. Then Dr. Rascher stripped off their skin and let the "leather" be used for such items as saddles, gloves, and ladies' handbags.[43] Goering had asked Himmler to send Jewish children from the camps to the medical institute at the University of

Strasbourg. Hundreds of them were injected with typhus (a deadly disease) and died.[44]

The French also had documents to show the brutality of Nazi occupation. One order from Hitler, called "Night and Fog," secretly shipped to German camps anyone committing an offense against the occupying power. Field Marshal Keitel relayed the following order to the Wehrmacht:

> In such cases penal servitude or even a hard labor sentence for life will be regarded as a sign of weakness. An effective and lasting deterrent can be achieved only by the death penalty or by taking measures which will leave the family and the population uncertain as to the fate of the offender. The deportation to Germany serves this purpose.[45]

Some twenty-nine thousand hostages had been shot in France. Forty thousand more had died under "protective custody" after Gestapo torture.[46]

Worst of all was the horror of the concentration camps. One of the most articulate witnesses was Madame Vaillant-Coutourier, a survivor of Auschwitz. She had seen women at the infirmary sterilized either by injections or by operation or with X rays. There was a very high mortality rate.[47]

The Eastern Soviet Case

On February 8, General Rudenko, the chief Soviet prosecutor, began presenting the case on human rights crimes in the East. There was even more suffering there than in Western Europe. Slavic people—in what is now Russia, Belorussia, Ukraine, Poland, the Czech Republic, Slovakia,

Serbia, and Slovenia—had been targeted for Hitler's worst treatment.

A Soviet state commission had estimated that four million houses had been burned down by the Nazis and huge quantities of food shipped to Germany, so that civilians starved to death.[48] At an August 1942 conference with Hitler, Sauckel had promised "to make Russian labor available for the fulfillment of the iron and coal program."[49] He had already supplied one million men for industry, another seven hundred thousand for agriculture. Two months later, Sauckel wrote Rosenberg that "two million [more] foreign laborers" had been ordered by Hitler.[50]

The Soviet prosecutor introduced a complaint from Rosenberg's office, which was in charge of occupied territories, to Field Marshal Keitel. It said that, "The fate of the Soviet prisoners of war [is] a tragedy of the greatest extent. Of 3,600,000 prisoners of war, only several hundred thousand are still able to work fully. A large part of them has starved, or died, because of the hazards of the weather. Thousands also died from spotted fever." When local farmers offered food to the starving prisoners,

> in the majority of cases the camp commanders have forbidden the civilian population to put food at the disposal of the prisoners and they have rather let them starve to death. . . . When prisoners of war could no longer keep up on the march because of hunger and exhaustion, they were shot before the eyes of the horrified civilian population, and the corpses were left.[51]

One witness described the mass murders by four mobile

killing squads. "Their principal task," he said, "was the annihilation of Jews, gypsies and political commissars."[52] Otto Ohlendorf, the commander of *Einsatzgruppe D*, was asked during his pretrial interrogation, "How many men, women and children did your group kill?" He shrugged and answered, with only the slightest hesitation, "Ninety thousand!"[53] Then Soviet judge Nikitchenko presented Ohlendorf with the following:

> **Question:** In your testimony you said that the Einsatz group had the object of annihilating the Jews and the commissars, is that correct?
>
> **Answer:** Yes.
>
> **Question:** And in what category did you consider the children? For what reason were the children massacred?
>
> **Answer:** The order was that the Jewish population should be totally exterminated.
>
> **Question:** Including the children?
>
> **Answer:** Yes.
>
> **Question:** Were all the Jewish children murdered?
>
> **Answer:** Yes.[54]

A British reporter for the *Daily Herald* wrote that a month of such horrifying testimony had numbed the courtroom. The Soviet prosecutor had been "speaking about the murder of millions of men, women and children. The court yawned." During a break, the reporters saw a Russian captain buying a snack at the cafeteria. "Suddenly he plunged his head into his hands and began to sob. 'Oh mother, sweet mother, dear father, why did they kill you?'. . . . Then with understanding in our hearts we went back to court."[55]

The defendants had been growing impatient during the months of prosecution. On March 8, 1946, their attorneys were ready to present their defense.

chapter six

THE CASE FOR THE DEFENSE

TRIAL CONTINUES—On March 8, 1946, the attorneys for the twenty-one defendants began making their case. The most important defendant was Goering, Hitler's designated successor and right-hand man. He had set up the first concentration camps, including Dachau, to imprison those who opposed Hitler. Then he became commander of the German air force, which played a key role in Nazi invasions. He also helped manage the wartime economy by stealing from occupied countries. Now his case was introduced by Otto Stahmer, a respected lawyer and judge, who was also a staunch Nazi from the city of Kiel. The British prosecutor had suggested him to Goering when his own choices were not available.

Witnesses for the Defense

First, Stahmer presented witnesses for the defense. Field Marshall Erhard Milch of the air force, for example, said that Goering had covered up Milch's background: his father had been a Jewish pharmacist. By inventing as his "real" father a minor Aryan nobleman, Goering may have saved Milch from a concentration camp. But Milch now wilted under Jackson's cross-examination. Wasn't he a member of a board that ran the slave labor program? he was asked. "I did not know that the workers who came from foreign countries had been deported," he answered. "We were told that they had been recruited on a voluntary basis."[1] Then British prosecutor G. D. Roberts asked him about his correspondence with Himmler, which mentioned medical "high pressure and cold water experiments" at Dachau that killed the human guinea pigs.[2] Milch lamely said he could not remember any such atrocities.

Birger Dahlerus was a Swedish engineer who had been employed by Goering's stepson. He testified that he had helped Goering make contacts in 1939 to prevent war with England. Under cross-examination by Sir David Maxwell-Fyfe, the chief British prosecutor, however, this testimony fell apart. Dahlerus agreed that Hitler had not wanted any last-minute compromise to avert war. His aim was simply "expanding our living space in the East."[3] When Goering had heard Hitler's call to arms, Dahlerus said he raised no objections.[4] Indeed, Goering acted "as if in some crazy state of intoxication" at the prospect of war, according to Dahlerus's published account.[5]

In other words, Goering's attempt to find a way to get British agreement to a settlement of German claims against Poland had no chance of working. It had not even involved regular German diplomats. And when Hitler pushed ahead with his plans to attack Poland, bringing its ally, England, into the war, Goering had enthusiastically supported him. The early contacts were evidently meant to hide Germany's aggressive plans.

After four days of witnesses, Goering took the stand on his own behalf. He had lost a lot of weight, thanks to the prison diet. At the interrogation center, he had also been weaned from his dependence on painkilling drugs. This left him in good physical and mental shape in the witness box. He was ready to take personal responsibility for the Nazi seizure of power and the buildup of the war machine. If anything, he wanted to magnify his own role at the top. Only when it came to war crimes did Goering plead ignorance or try to explain them away.

There could be no talk of a Nazi conspiracy, Goering argued, because he alone had the closest possible ties with Hitler. "Therefore, at best, only the Führer and I could have conspired. There is definitely no question of the others."[6] It was preposterous to accuse generals like Keitel of waging wars of aggression. Political leaders decided whether or not to wage war, and the military were duty bound to follow.[7] Goering thus turned away the prosecution's fire from his fellow defendants. He saw in the trial "his last chance of once more playing a leading part and being admired by a worldwide audience."[8] As to Luftwaffe attacks on Warsaw, Poland, and Coventry, England, Goering's witness, Colonel Albert Kesselring, said these were legitimate military targets. The bombing of Rotterdam in the Netherlands was regrettably due to a failure of radio communication.[9]

Regarding anti-Semitic measures, Goering said he was more humane than propaganda chief Goebbels. Did he cooperate with Gestapo boss Himmler? "That I requested inmates of concentration camps for the aviation industry is correct, and it is in my opinion quite natural because I was, at that time, not familiar with the details of the concentration camps."[10] Did the attack on Russia leave the inhabitants starving to feed the Wehrmacht? That could not have been intended, he said. "It is impossible for one soldier on the one

During the trials, the defendants were housed in the prison building (shown here) behind the Palace of Justice.

side to eat so much that on the other side there is not enough left for three times that number. The fact is moreover that the population did not starve."[11]

Goering was an impressive witness on his own behalf. He tried to minimize the war crimes he was accused of, yet he enlarged his own place in history. But he introduced a Nazi slant to the accounts the prosecution had given. If he did not know of the murders at concentration camps, it was because he chose not to inform himself at high-level meetings. And it had been obvious that the food supply from Russia was not used just for the Wehrmacht but for German civilians at home. That explained the years of Russian famine starvation under Nazi rule.

Jackson's Skills Questioned

These discrepancies had to be revealed in cross-examination. On March 18, Jackson led off, but soon his lack of trial experience became apparent. For the next two days, he repeatedly mixed up the proper names and titles of people mentioned in documents, and Goering had to correct him. For example, Jackson asked about the head of the German police, Kurt Daluege, "Who, by the way, was he?"[12] He should have known that this man had been held and questioned at Nuremberg not long before.

Soon Jackson became irritated at Goering's lengthy answers to his overly general questions. "Can you not answer yes or no?" he asked. "Did you then know, at the same time that you knew that the war was lost, that the German cities could not successfully be defended against air attacks by the enemy?"[13] Jackson's point did not seem to relate to any of the charges against Goering. It was not his knowledge but his illegal actions that were on trial.

In further questioning, Jackson misstated the names, dates, and organizations in documents in evidence. Goering kept correcting him in a way that infuriated Jackson. He also went off on tangents, while Jackson kept asking for yes or no answers. The judges, despite Jackson's objections, allowed the defendant to complete his answers. Jackson grew even angrier.

During one exchange with Goering, Jackson complained to the judges,

> This witness, it seems to me, is adopting, and has adopted, in the witness box and in the dock, an arrogant and contemptuous attitude toward the Tribunal which is giving him the trial which he never gave a living soul, nor dead ones either. I respectfully submit that the witness be instructed to make notes, if he wishes, of his explanations, but that he be required to answer my questions and reserve his explanations for his counsel to bring out.[14]

The judges adjourned the trial for the day at that point, but the next morning Jackson renewed his criticism of Goering's long-winded answers.[15] The judges refused to require yes or no replies.

Yet, when Jackson returned to the cross-examination, Goering had trouble explaining away his central role. For example in a meeting following November 9, 1938, known as *Kristallnacht* (the "night of broken glass" for shattered windows in Jewish shops and synagogues), had he not told the ruthless Gestapo chief Reinhard Heydrich, "I wish you had killed two hundred Jews instead of destroying such valuables"? Goering snapped, "Yes, this was said in a moment of bad temper and excitement."[16]

Later, Jackson asked Goering about his order of July 16, 1941, telling Himmler and Heydrich to finish clearing Jews out of Nazi-occupied lands. Goering, relying on his knowledge of English, could only point out that the translation "final solution" should have read "a total solution of the Jewish question," as if that made a major difference.[17] Despite these occasional points for the prosecution, Goering was still succeeding in holding his own.

But back in his cell, Goering told another defendant, "Accept the fact that your life is lost." The other defendants should be ready to "die a martyr's death" like Goering. They could be consoled knowing that "some day the German people will rise again and acknowledge us as heroes, and our bones will be moved to marble caskets, in a national shrine."[18]

The British Cross-Examine

Sir David Maxwell-Fyfe now took over the cross-examination. As a brilliant trial lawyer, he would not give Goering the chance to dodge questions as Jackson had. He asked about one of Goering's orders that let recaptured Soviet prisoners be turned over to the Gestapo for hard labor or to be killed. When Goering said this was not "exactly correct," Maxwell-Fyfe had him read a key sentence from a document, "If a Soviet prisoner of war is returned to the

An American guard looks inside the prison cell of Hermann Goering. All areas except the toilet were watched around the clock to prevent Goering from committing suicide.

camp, he has to be handed to the nearest service station of the Secret State Police [Gestapo]."[19] Goering could not deny it.

Next Maxwell-Fyfe discussed the death camps in which millions of Jews had been murdered. Even Hitler had known nothing about this, Goering insisted. How could the killing of so many millions of Jews have been kept from him? Maxwell-Fyfe asked. "I am still of the opinion that the Führer did not know . . .," Goering said.[20]

Maxwell-Fyfe then cited notes from a meeting on April 17, 1943. Admiral Nicholas Horthy, the Hungarian regent, asked Hitler and von Ribbentrop what he should do with Hungary's Jews. Von Ribbentrop said that they should be "exterminated or taken to concentration camps." Hitler then went into a tirade claiming that the Jews had brought "the most terrible misery and decay" to Hungary. "They had to be treated like tuberculosis . . ., with which a healthy body may become infected. . . . Nations which do not rid themselves of Jews perish."[21] Still Goering kept insisting that neither he nor Hitler knew of the policy to exterminate Jews. He said he was aware only of "a policy of emigration, not liquidation of the Jews."[22]

How could Goering, who founded the first concentration camps, now disown all such murder factories? How could he admit using camp inmates for war industry and not know in what condition they arrived? Finally, how could he maintain his loyalty to the dead Führer but deny that his policies included mass killings of Jews and other people? Goering may have had better stage presence than his fellow defendants, yet the written records did not support his pleas of ignorance.

Some of the most damaging evidence of war crimes was introduced against Field Marshal Keitel. As head of the high command for five years, he signed hundreds of orders from Hitler. Keitel did not deny that "such orders often contain deviations from existing international law."[23] But he claimed that, "In carrying out these thankless and difficult tasks, I had to fulfill my duty . . . often acting against the inner voice of my conscience and against my own convictions. I was a loyal and obedient soldier of my Führer."[24]

Prosecutor Maxwell-Fyfe pressed Keitel for details. Had he not issued the "Night and Fog" decree, which spread terror through the Nazi-occupied lands? Had not the Wehrmacht turned over to the security police tens of thousands who vanished without a trace? Keitel distanced himself from "the full and monstrous tragedy" that, he said, he had only realized now. He had not meant this order to be "applied universally by the police," resulting in "the horrible fact of the existence of whole camps full of people deported through this [Night and Fog] procedure."[25]

Maxwell-Fyfe moved on to the "commando order," which sentenced to death any captured Allied raiders. "How did you tolerate all these young men being murdered, one after the other, without making any protest?" he asked Keitel.[26] The field marshal claimed he had not personally carried out the orders, but he admitted, "I know that these incidents occurred and I know the consequences."[27] Maxwell-Fyfe pressed Keitel. Why had neither he nor other generals, as the bearers of the Prussian military tradition, had "the courage to stand up and oppose cold-blooded murder?" Keitel could only confess, "I did not do it; I made no further objection to these things. I can say no more. . . ."[28]

Keitel's basic honesty only aroused the anger of some of the other defendants. Goering was angry with Keitel for admitting too much.[29] Admiral Doenitz thought Keitel had been "too weak. As long as he did go so far as to sign those orders he could at least have said that the Russians did just

The prison chapel at Nuremberg (shown here) was visited regularly by sixteen of the prisoners. Facing death sentences, they hoped that religion would provide salvation. Others, such as Goering, used religion as an excuse to leave their cell.

as much and worse."[30] The remaining defendants used similar strategies to Goering's or Keitel's. Some denied that they had known or taken part in the acts they were accused of; they tried to minimize their misdeeds or said they had to follow orders. Others admitted at least partial responsibility. A few even expressed remorse. Some of the defense attorneys argued capably for their clients. Most of them, however, made it clear that they had no sympathy for the horrors shown in prosecution documents and films.

Hess, Hitler's former deputy, relied on a variation of the insanity defense. He was suffering from amnesia, his lawyer argued. Indeed, he had flown to England before the war against Russia led to the worst Nazi measures. But he stood accused of following Hitler in persecuting Jews and Poles. He would not take the stand. But Hess's lawyer said that his client:

> assumes responsibility for all orders and directives which he issued. . . . For these reasons he does not desire to be defended against any charges which refer to the internal affairs of Germany as a sovereign state.[31]

The psychologist, Gilbert, seemed to have no doubt that Hess's memory span was less than one day.[32]

Now it was the turn of Joachim von Ribbentrop, Hitler's foreign minister. His attorney, Martin Horn, also complained that his client's mental condition was worsening day by day. Von Ribbentrop denied that he had attended meetings at which he was known to have been present. He also imagined doing things that appeared fictional. Horn asked the court's permission to avoid questioning von Ribbentrop. Instead he wanted to ask von Ribbentrop whether or not he agreed with prepared answers. The judges denied the request. They asked two doctors to examine von Ribbentrop. They reported that he was not ill, just paralyzed by fear of being questioned in public.[33]

The first defense witness was Baron Steengracht von Moyland, von Ribbentrop's state secretary. At first he tried to shift the blame from his former boss. When asked about von Ribbentrop's responsibility for anti-Semitic policies, Steengracht said, "The Foreign Office could not exercise general control since all anti-Jewish questions were principally dealt with in Rosenberg's office."[34] Then he stopped defending the foreign minister, saying,

> I should like to make a distinction between the real instincts of von Ribbentrop and what he said when he was under Hitler's influence. . . . He was completely hypnotized by Hitler and then became his tool. . . . He followed blindly the orders given by Hitler.[35]

Things did not go any better with the next witness, Margaret Blank, von Ribbentrop's longtime secretary. She also remarked on von Ribbentrop's loyalty to Hitler. "When speaking of Hitler to his subordinates he did so with the greatest admiration." What if he disagreed? "In cases of differences of opinion between himself and the Führer," Herr von Ribbentrop gave in. Once a decision had been made by Adolf Hitler there was no more criticism afterward.[36]

When von Ribbentrop finally took the stand, his answers did not help his case. He claimed he had never intended the Jews any harm. The French prosecutor quoted from minutes of the April 1943 meeting between Hitler and the Hungarian regent, Admiral Horthy. "The Foreign Minister declared that the Jews were either to be exterminated or sent to concentration camps. There was no other solution."[37] Had he said that? Not in those words, was the answer. Justice Lawrence now asked if he had said that Jews should be taken to concentration camps. Von Ribbentrop answered, "I consider it possible that such may have been the case," but he argued that the minutes were not quite accurate. The prosecutor now asked if he had not supported Hitler's policy to deport all Jews. Now von Ribbentrop admitted, "As his faithful follower, I adhered to the Führer's orders even in this field."[38]

Later, back in their cells, the other defendants commented on von Ribbentrop's lack of an intelligent argument and what that implied about his performance as foreign minister. Goering said, "What a pitiful spectacle! If I had only known, I would have gone into our foreign policy a little more myself." Former ambassador von Papen added, "Ach, there's no use letting that fool talk any more—he has convicted himself already. They might as well go on with the next case."[39]

On April 11, 1946, Kaltenbrunner began his defense. He had succeeded the dreaded Heydrich as chief of the Reich main security office, which took orders directly from Hitler. Even though his attorney, Kurt Kauffmann, had been a Nazi and served in the Wehrmacht, he questioned Kaltenbrunner to get at the truth. For example, he asked his client about Hitler's 1941 "commissar order," which asked that Communists among Russian prisoners of war be "eliminated." Kauffmann said, "It can be assumed obviously that you, too, must have been informed about this extremely grave situation, which was inhuman and prohibited by international law, does it not?" Incredibly, Kaltenbrunner replied, "I was not informed of it."[40]

Kaltenbrunner contradicted the evidence from documents, the testimony of witnesses, and even photographs. As mentioned in Chapter 5, he denied that he had ever visited the infamous Mauthausen camp in Austria. Yet a camp guard testified that Kaltenbrunner and von Schirach had toured the gas chamber.[41] Kaltenbrunner had even been photographed there. He had also watched inmates being hurled down the stone quarry to their death.[42] A former camp inmate testified that he had been lying ill in the freezing cold, without medical treatment, when "Kaltenbrunner walked through the barracks [and] . . . saw everything, must have seen everything."[43]

Another witness, who had been a high Gestapo official, said that Kaltenbrunner had approved executing suspects in what was called "special treatment." Not at all, said Kaltenbrunner. He claimed that "special treatment" really meant sending prisoners to a mountain resort where they were given "nine times the ration of the ordinary German during the war." According to Kaltenbrunner, they even enjoyed a daily bottle of champagne.[44] The court was stunned by such outrageous lies.

Another Gestapo official said that only Kaltenbrunner could put suspects under "protective custody." Kaltenbrunner denied signing thousands of orders bearing

Ernst Kaltenbrunner, the senior surviving official of the SS, stands to answer a prosecution question from the defense bench.

his signature. His attorney, Kauffmann, suggested that such a denial "is not very credible. It is a monstrosity that the office chief should not know that such orders were signed with his name."[45] This time Kaltenbrunner's response was that Gestapo chief Heinrich Mueller must have signed his name for years without permission.

Finally, Colonel Rudolf Hoess, the commandant of the Auschwitz death camp (not to be confused with the defendant Rudolf Hess) testified that three million Jews had died there as of December 1943—two million by being gassed, the rest from disease and illness. The exact number of people killed at Auschwitz may never be known. One recent estimate (on the low side) gives the following figures: 960,000 Jews (with hundreds of thousands more suffering from the effects of starvation, disease, and slavery); 74,000 non-Jewish Poles; 21,000 Roma and Sinti (gypsies); 15,000 Soviet prisoners of war; and 12,000 other Christians.[46] Kaltenbrunner had "often conferred personally and frequently communicated orally and in writing concerning concentration camps. . . . The 'final solution' of the Jewish question meant the complete extermination of all Jews in Europe."[47] At the Treblinka camp, "children of tender years were invariably exterminated since by reason of their youth they were unable to work."[48]

Later the prison psychologist talked to Hoess. Had he ever asked himself whether the Jews he had murdered were guilty or deserved such a fate? Hoess struggled to come up with an answer, saying, "Don't you see we SS men were not supposed to think about these things; it never occurred to us.

And besides, it was already taken for granted that the Jews were to blame for everything."[49]

Defendants like Kaltenbrunner posed few legal problems for the judges. But how would they decide the guilt or innocence of others who had fought the war mainly according to accepted rules? Admiral Karl Doenitz, for instance, was accused of telling his submarine commanders not to rescue survivors of the ships they sank.[50] Yet witnesses from the German navy said that they had never fired at shipwrecked sailors.[51] A turning point in the Doenitz case came when the defense attorney was allowed to write to Admiral Chester W. Nimitz, commander of the United States fleet in the Pacific, asking him how he conducted submarine warfare. Nimitz stated that his submarines were under orders to attack merchant ships without warning. They also did not pick up survivors if it put their own ships in danger.[52] Doenitz's actions now did not appear so criminal, since he had done the same thing that the United States Navy had routinely done.

Defendants Make Trial Statements

By August 31, 1946, the prosecution and defense cases had concluded. Now each of the defendants was given fifteen minutes to make his final statements. Some, like Hjalmar Schacht, who had been president of the German national bank that financed Hitler's schemes, used this last chance to proclaim their innocence. Schacht said,

> At the conclusion of this trial I stand shaken to the very depths of my soul by the unspeakable suffering which I tried

to prevent with all my personal efforts and with all attainable means, but which in the end I failed to prevent—not through my fault.[53]

Labor chief Fritz Sauckel said he had been wrong to worship Hitler. "In all humility and reverence, I bow before the victims and the fallen of all nations, and before the misfortune and suffering of my own people, with whom alone I must measure my fate."[54]

Goering said, "I wish to state expressly that I condemn these terrible mass murders to the utmost, and cannot understand them in the least." But he denied that he had ever "decreed the murder of a single individual at any time. . . . The only motive which guided me was my ardent love for my people, its happiness, its freedom, and its life."[55]

It was now up to the judges to weigh the arguments by the prosecution and the defense of the individual defendants and the six Nazi organizations.

chapter seven

THE JUDGES DECIDE

VERDICT—After the last of the defendants' speeches, presiding judge Geoffrey Lawrence announced that the trial would adjourn (recess) until September 23, when the court would announce the verdicts. But a week before that date, another announcement put off the judgment until September 30. It implied that the judges were having trouble reaching agreement.

Agreement Among Judges a Problem

Long after the trial ended, it became clear how difficult it was for the eight judges to come to an agreement. Some of them hinted at these problems in their writings. But the fullest account emerged from the private papers of Francis Biddle, the senior American judge. Several boxes of his papers are now available to researchers in the special collections of Syracuse University library in upstate New York.

The Biddle papers revealed that the judges began deliberating toward the end of June 1946, when the defense arguments still had two months to go. The judges were deeply divided on the following three issues:

1. Questions of law, such as whether or not to rely on Count One of the indictment, regarding conspiracy;

2. The guilt or innocence of about half of the defendants, who had played relatively minor roles in the Nazi state or had not been directly involved in war crimes;

3. How to determine the common guilt of those who had belonged to six Nazi organizations. In addition to these major points, there was also disagreement on secondary questions, such as whether senior military figures should be executed by shooting or hanging.

All the sessions of the eight judges—two each from Great Britain, the United States, France, and the Soviet Union—were held in strict secrecy, with only two interpreters added. When they first met on June 27, 1946, British judge Norman Birkett had already prepared a draft opinion. French judge Donnedieu de Vabres thought this draft was too long. But his sharpest argument turned against the use of the conspiracy charge, that is making a secret plan to commit a crime. De Vabres said that this concept from Anglo-Saxon law was unknown in international law. It should be dropped, since it was "ex post facto," in other words, applying to acts that had not been illegal at the time. Charges should be directed at specific criminal acts, so that "the crime absorbs the conspiracy."[1]

The argument impressed American judge Biddle. He asked Herbert Wechsler, one of his assistants who had returned to teach law at Columbia University, to comment. He told Wechsler that the judges were now "engaged in making [a] preliminary draft of an opinion (in great secrecy), though we have not yet come to consider any individual guilt."[2] At another session, on August 14, 1946, de Vabres proposed dropping the conspiracy charge. He was joined by Robert Falco, the other French judge, who said that conspiracy was too hard to define; it would be better simply to stick to the facts of the case.[3]

But at the next day's session, both Birkett and Russian judge Nikitchenko argued against dropping the essence of the first count. "Do you want to acquit the Nazi regime?" asked Birkett. Nikitchenko said that conspiracy was needed as a separate charge; without it, defendants like the broadcaster Fritzsche would slip away. In any case, he added, the charter of the court had knowingly introduced a number of new concepts into international law.[4]

On August 19, 1946, John J. Parker, the second American judge, said that the conspiracy charge had already been proven. If it were to be dropped now, it would undercut the case against the six indicted Nazi organizations.[5] At this meeting, Biddle said that the charge was also needed against the banker Schacht. In subsequent sessions, only the French judges remained opposed to this charge. On September 6, 1946, Biddle (using Wechsler's advice) now suggested the following compromise: conspiracy would be limited to waging aggressive war, not to war crimes or crimes against humanity.[6]

But when did such a conspiracy begin? The prosecutors had said it started with the founding of the Nazi party. The judges found the start of the conspiracy at two military conferences—on May 11, 1937, and November 23, 1939—at which Hitler had planned seizing Austria and Czechoslovakia, then attacking other countries. Goering, von Neurath, and military leaders had been present. There

Four of the Allied prosecutors are shown here on August 30, 1946, the day of their summations: France's Champetier de Ribes, Britain's Sir David Maxwell-Fyfe, the United States's Thomas Dodd, and the Soviet Union's General Roman A. Rudenko.

had not been "a single master conspiracy between the defendants," the judges agreed, but "many separate plans."[7]

As the judges broke down the conspiracy charge, fewer and fewer defendants could be found guilty of association in planning Hitler's aggressive wars. All twenty-one defendants had been accused of conspiracy, but only eight were finally found guilty of it, in the sense of having knowingly planned a crime. It took the judges more than twenty meetings to reach a majority on all the cases. That meant that of the four senior judges who could vote, at least three had to find common ground to convict. A two-to-two vote amounted to an acquittal.[8]

Definition of Aggression Needed

If conspiracy was to be used only as it related to waging aggressive war, the judges still had to work out a definition of aggression. De Vabres said that even the United Nations could not agree on a definition, so it was better to stick to examples.[9] Did the Nazi attack on Greece qualify? Parker said perhaps, although "the English had actually got in first."[10] In other words, the defendants could claim that the Wehrmacht had attacked Greece only because British troops were stationed there.

Would the Nazi seizure of Austria be considered aggression? But that country welcomed its annexation into Germany. How about Czechoslovakia, which Germany seized with British and French consent at the Munich conference of September 1938? Judges' assistants said that former Foreign Minister von Ribbentrop had been "a knowing participant in the plan to occupy Czechoslovakia by threat of invasion, if possible, by actual invasion, if necessary."[11] Biddle was not satisfied, saying, "But this isn't alleged as an aggressive war."[12]

Finally, the western judges wrestled with the problem of Poland. The Germans had occupied the western half of that country, after agreeing with the Soviets that they could take the eastern half. This followed a secret appendix to the 1939 Nazi-Soviet pact. Russian judge Nikitchenko kept insisting that no reference be made to this "secret agreement."[13] Later, both Russian judges said they could not understand the problems of the others—after all, everyone knew that the Nazis had a common "plan to dominate the world."[14]

Determining Degree of Criminal Responsibility

The second problem for the judges was determining the degree of criminal responsibility for each defendant. At their September 2, 1946, session, the judges concurred on the first ten cases. They agreed on the guilt of Goering, Hess, von Ribbentrop, Keitel, Rosenberg, Frank, Kaltenbrunner, Jodl, Seyss-Inquart and (without him being present for the trial) Bormann. When it came to Streicher, Biddle noted, "I blurt out that I think it's preposterous to hold a little Jew baiter as a conspirator because he was a friend of Hitler, or a Gauleiter, or a Nazi."[15] His case was to be decided later.

The initial session finished by agreeing on the guilt of Sauckel, with split votes on Funk, Speer, and von Neurath. These and the rest of the cases took four more meetings of the judges to resolve. By September 10, there were only a few individual dissents on guilty verdicts with death sentences for Kaltenbrunner, Keitel, von Ribbentrop, Rosenberg, Frank, Frick, Streicher, Sauckel, Seyss-Inquart, and Bormann. Hess was to be given a life sentence. The other cases took two more rounds of bargaining among the judges. The final decisions about who was to get a death sentence or jail time never revealed the weeks of arguments that had come before.

Finally, the Russian judges were the only holdouts in the acquittal of these three defendants: Schacht, von Papen, and Fritzsche. Funk and Admiral Raeder were given life sentences; Speer and von Schirach twenty years; von Neurath fifteen; and Doenitz ten.[16] The von Papen and Schacht opinions swung back and forth, but ended in a two-two tie. The Doenitz decision pitted Biddle, arguing for acquittal, against the three other judges. Then, after sentencing the senior admiral, Raeder, to life, all the judges agreed that Doenitz, his junior, should receive a lesser sentence.[17]

Like some of the individual judgments, those on the six indicted Nazi organizations resulted in compromises. At first, the Russian judges wanted them all condemned, while Biddle argued to "throw them all out—a shocking thing this group crime."[18] It took several long sessions to show that a majority of the judges wanted only to convict the SS, Gestapo, SD, and top Nazi party leaders. All of these had members who joined voluntarily in war crimes and crimes against humanity.[19] The other organizations—the SA, general staff/high command, and the Reich cabinet—were too insignificant during World War II, when Hitler's regime was guilty of its worst excesses.

Did these compromises result in justice? In 1992, American Assistant Prosecutor Telford Taylor looked back at the trial and had some doubts. For example, Taylor found little merit in the judges' "hasty and unthinking" conviction of Streicher.[20] For this he blamed the American judges, versed in the Bill of Rights with its guarantee of free speech. He also found the logic of de Vabres, the senior French

Albert Speer, director of the Nazi armament program, walks into the courtroom (through door at right). Other defendants in the front row are (left to right) Hermann Goering, Rudolf Hess, Joachim von Ribbentrop, and Wilhelm Keitel.

judge, "baffling."[21] Taylor said he almost never wanted to acquit anyone, yet shrank from imposing a severe sentence.

British journalist Dan van der Vat thought the court had been wrong to accept the senility of Gustav Krupp as a reason to drop his case. After all, he was far from the oldest or most feeble defendant.[22] He further thought that Speer outsmarted the judges by exploiting the western-Soviet split in the court staff.[23] It has also been pointed out that Sauckel was hanged for recruiting slave labor but that Speer served only twenty years for *using* that same labor force in his factories.[24]

At first, the judges did not agree on the method of executing the defendants who were sentenced to death. Biddle, for example, wanted to "hang Keitel and shoot Jodl."[25] The military men among the defendants had pleaded for shooting as the honorable way out. Hanging was seen as a shameful punishment reserved for traitors. Soon, all the judges agreed on hanging the condemned men, though it was not clear why or how they came to this conclusion.

Verdicts Announced

The lengthy decision of the tribunal was ready on September 30, 1946. After 453 sessions, the judges were ready to announce their verdict. They took turns reading the 170 pages over two days.[26] First, the courtroom crowded with the world press corps heard a history of the rise of Nazism and a summary of the evidence. Then the judges discussed the conspiracy charge—planning "aggressive war . . . the supreme international crime."[27] A list of countries attacked by the Wehrmacht was given chronologically, together with an account of broken treaties.

The first day's presentation ended with an outline of the case against the six organizations. The Nazi leadership was found guilty of persecuting Jews and enslaving the citizens of occupied countries, the Gestapo and SD of participating in the killing of Jews, and the SS of running the concentration camps.[28] The SA, however, was merely a group of "unimportant Nazi hangers-on" after 1936, the Reich cabinet ceased functioning after 1937, and the general staff and high command were not distinct "criminal organizations," as defined by the charter.[29]

The October 1, 1946, session began with the findings for each defendant on the various counts. The four voting judges began by finding Goering guilty on all counts. Then came the verdicts for the other twenty defendants, plus Bormann who was found guilty of war crimes and crimes against humanity despite the fact that he was never actually present at the trial. After the first ten defendants had been convicted, the acquittal of Schacht because of "reasonable doubt" came as a surprise. Von Papen and Fritzsche were also found not guilty. Next a mixed verdict acquitted Doenitz of planning, but convicted him of waging aggressive war. The von Schirach verdict was also split: innocent of preparing war through the Hitler Youth but guilty of deporting sixty thousand Jews from Vienna to Poland in 1940—a crime against humanity.

The other verdicts–against Raeder, Sauckel, Jodl, Seyss-Inquart, Frank, Rosenberg, and Funk—appeared routine.

Speer, however, was found guilty only of "his participation in the slave labor program." A deciding factor was that he prevented needless destruction of factories in occupied countries, even sabotaging Hitler's "scorched earth program." This scheme left only wasteland behind the retreating German armies. Von Neurath was convicted of all four counts, but the judges noted that he had interceded with the SD to secure the release of imprisoned Czechs.

After the lunch break, the defendants heard their sentences. Twelve of them were given the death penalty: Goering, von Ribbentrop, Kaltenbrunner, Rosenberg, Frank, Frick, Streicher, Seyss-Inquart, Sauckel, Keitel, Jodl, and the absent Bormann. Seven were given prison sentences, with Hess, Funk, and Raeder getting life terms. Shorter sentences were given to von Schirach and Speer (twenty years), von Neurath (fifteen), and Doenitz (ten).

Later that afternoon, psychologist Gilbert observed the men's reactions. Jodl complained, "Death—by hanging! That, at least, I did not deserve." Von Ribbentrop said, "Death!—Death! Now I won't be able to write my beautiful memoirs." Frank was more stoic, "I deserved it and I expected it, as I've always told you. I am glad that I have had the chance to defend myself and to think things over in the last few months." Speer laughed about his twenty-year sentence: "Well, that's fair enough. They couldn't have given me a lighter sentence, considering the facts, and I can't complain."[30] The three men who were found not guilty were elated. But for the moment, with angry demonstrators outside, they decided to stay in prison.

Armored cars patrol the grounds of the Palace of Justice during the verdict days, September 30 and October 1, 1946.

Soviet judge Nikitchenko filed a lengthy dissent (opinion in disagreement), even though he had signed the common decision. This dissent argued that all three of the defendants found not guilty—Schacht, von Papen, and Fritzsche—should have been found guilty, and that Hess deserved the death sentence instead of prison. Nikitchenko also disagreed with the innocent verdicts for the Reich cabinet, the general staff, and the high command. In the end, this made no difference, though his public disagreement upset his western colleagues.[31]

Appeals Filed

The court's charter had provided that appeals could be filed by the defendants to the Allied military government. All defendants, except Kaltenbrunner and Speer, submitted appeals. The attorney for Frank asked that his sentence be lessened to life imprisonment, while Streicher's lawyer argued that his client had not conducted aggressive war. Goering, Keitel, and Jodl simply asked for death by shooting instead of hanging. Jackson had sent a letter to the War Department seeking to limit any appeals. In any case, the generals in charge of the four occupied zones of Germany rejected all the appeals by October 10, 1946.[32]

Preparations were now made to execute the eleven condemned men by hanging in the prison gymnasium on the morning of October 15, 1946. When the guards came to Goering's cell the night before, however, they found him already dead of cyanide poisoning. He had managed to conceal a tiny glass vial of poison, perhaps underneath the toilet seat. The other ten men were hanged as scheduled. Streicher, defiant to the end, screamed "Heil Hitler" as he was led to his death.[33] Before dawn, their corpses were taken to Dachau, the former concentration camp. All eleven were cremated in the ovens "that had claimed so many lives" of their victims.[34] The ashes were collected and secretly thrown into the *Contwentzbach*, a small stream near Munich.

More Trials Follow

The trial of "major war criminals" by the four Allied powers was over. There would be a dozen more Nuremberg trials in the next three years. They would deal with about 190 defendants. But the Cold War had split the western Allies from the Soviet Union. So the subsequent cases—of doctors who had conducted "experiments" on concentration camp inmates, of SS officers who had commanded the *Einsatzgruppen* killing squads, of Krupp armaments executives, and others—were run solely by the United States.

The defendants who had been given jail sentences were eventually taken to the huge Spandau prison in West Berlin. Raeder, Funk, and von Neurath were released early because of failing health. Doenitz, von Schirach, and Speer served out their sentences. Hess remained at Spandau as the sole prisoner from 1966 until 1987. Then at age ninety-three, he committed suicide by choking himself with an electric wire. The Soviet member of the Allied council had refused to agree to release him earlier.

Lessons for the Future

Were there lessons to be learned from the Nuremberg trial? Some legal scholars said that it amounted to "victor's justice," as Goering had charged.[35] The Allies obtained a last measure of revenge, but the Germans were too steeped in mass destruction after the war to need any further proof discrediting Hitler's regime. Other observers note that the impact of Nuremberg lives on in these four ways:

1. Its evidence of "crimes against humanity" has inspired museums and memorials to the Holocaust. German schoolchildren visit concentration camps like Dachau. The United States Holocaust Memorial Museum in Washington, D.C., attracts record numbers of tourists each year. The forty-two volumes of Nuremberg testimony disprove the claims of those who refuse to believe that the Holocaust occurred.

2. The United Nations supported the judgment at Nuremberg on December 11, 1946, and adopted its principles. These ideals are also found in the Convention on Genocide, adopted by the United Nations in 1948, as well as in the 1950 Convention for the Protection of Human Rights and Basic Freedoms. They are now part of international law.

3. Since 1995, two war crimes tribunals have operated in The Hague, the capital of the Netherlands. The United Nations set them up under its charter to prosecute war crimes in Rwanda and in the former Yugoslavia. They are different from the Nuremberg Trial, which was a military court of four Allied nations that won World War II. Louise Arbour, the

chief prosecutor, filed indictments in May 1999 against Serbian president Slobodan Milosovic and four other top leaders for war crimes in the province of Kosovo. They, in turn, argued that this was a civil, not an international, war—therefore, outside the tribunal's jurisdiction.

4. Besides courts for specific war crimes, many nations have been proposing a permanent international criminal court. President Bill Clinton said that he wanted to see such a court set up by the year 2000.[36] Yet, delegates from the United States to the Rome

The twenty-one defendants at the Nuremberg Trials (left to right, front row): Hermann Goering, Rudolf Hess, Joachim von Ribbentrop, Wilhelm Keitel, Ernst Kaltenbrunner, Alfred Rosenberg, Hans Frank, Wilhelm Frick, Julius Streicher, Walter Funk, and Hjalmar Schacht, (rear) Karl Doenitz, Erich Raeder, Baldur von Schirach, Fritz Sauckel, Alfred Jodl, Franz von Papen, Arthur Seyss-Inquart, Albert Speer, Constantin von Neurath, and Hans Fritzsche.

Conference that considered such a court in June 1998 tried to limit ways in which cases could be referred to it, such as only when a state's own "legal system has collapsed or is unavailable."[37] Then, cases could be referred only by the Security Council or United Nations member states, not by an independent prosecutor. The United States Senate is unlikely to approve a treaty that would expose American troops to prosecution for carrying out peacekeeping missions.[38]

The most lasting effect of the Nuremberg Trial may be that it set a fair and impartial standard to judge war crimes. It tried to avoid the wartime feelings of revenge, which would have led to collective judgments against the whole German people or at least to the execution of all the accused. Finally, it established the concept of "crimes against humanity" in international law.

No matter where they occur, such crimes have now become the concern of the whole international community. There still is no simple, direct way to bring those who commit these crimes to justice. For example, only twenty of the ninety-one Serbs and Croats indicted for war crimes in Yugoslavia have been brought to The Hague for trial so far.[39] But anyone suspected of war crimes cannot rest easy, knowing that all members of the United Nations are obligated to arrest that person. War criminals can never be certain that sooner or later they will not have to defend themselves before an international court, as did the Nazi leaders at Nuremberg.

Indictments and Verdicts at Nuremberg

Count 1: Conspiracy to commit the crimes in Counts 2, 3, and 4.

Count 2: Crimes against peace—by waging "wars of aggression" and "wars in violation of international treaties."

Count 3: War crimes—by violating the traditional laws and rules of warfare.

Count 4: Crimes against humanity—by murder, extermination, and "persecution on political, religious, or racial grounds."

Defendant:	Indicted under Counts:	Verdict:	Sentence:
Hermann Goering	1, 2, 3, 4	Guilty 1–4	Hanging*
Joachim von Ribbentrop	1, 2, 3, 4	Guilty 1–4	Hanging
Rudolf Hess	1, 2, 3, 4	Guilty 1, 2	Life
Ernst Kaltenbrunner	1, 3, 4	Guilty 3, 4	Hanging
Alfred Rosenberg	1, 2, 3, 4	Guilty 1–4	Hanging
Hans Frank	1, 3, 4	Guilty 3, 4	Hanging
Martin Bormann	1, 3, 4	Guilty 3, 4	Hanging**
Wilhelm Frick	1, 2, 3, 4	Guilty 2–4	Hanging
Fritz Sauckel	1, 2, 3, 4	Guilty 3, 4	Hanging
Albert Speer	1, 2, 3, 4	Guilty 3, 4	20 years
Walter Funk	1, 2, 3, 4	Guilty 2–4	Life
Hjalmar Schacht	1, 2	Acquitted	N/A
Franz von Papen	1, 2	Acquitted	N/A
Constantin von Neurath	1, 2, 3, 4	Guilty 1–4	15 years
Baldur von Schirach	1, 4	Guilty 4	20 years
Arthur Seyss-Inquart	1, 2, 3, 4	Guilty 2–4	Hanging
Julius Streicher	1, 4	Guilty 4	Hanging
Wilhelm Keitel	1, 2, 3, 4	Guilty 1–4	Hanging
Alfred Jodl	1, 2, 3, 4	Guilty 1–4	Hanging
Erich Raeder	1, 2, 3	Guilty 1–3	Life
Karl Doenitz	1, 2, 3	Guilty 2, 3	10 years
Hans Fritzsche	1, 3, 4	Acquitted	N/A

*Committed suicide before the execution. **Sentenced without being there. He was never found alive.

Chapter Notes

TMWC = Trial of the Major War Criminals Before the International Military Tribunal, Nuremberg, November 14, 1945–October 1, 1946 (Nuremberg: International Military Tribunal, 1947)

Chapter 1. Liberating a Concentration Camp

All quoted material is taken from the author's interview with Walter Pauk, July 20, 1994.

Chapter 2. Would the War Criminals be Prosecuted?

1. W. H. Lawrence, "President Warns Atrocities of Axis Will Be Avenged," *The New York Times*, August 22, 1942, p. 1.

2. Ibid., p. 4.

3. Ibid.

4. *Trial of the Major War Criminals Before the International Military Tribunal, Nuremberg, November 14, 1945–October 1, 1946* (Nuremberg: International Military Tribunal, 1947), vol. VIII, p. 417.

5. United States Department of State, *International Conference on Military Trials* (Washington, D.C.: Government Printing Office, 1949), p. 12.

6. Henry L. Stimson and McGeorge Bundy, *On Active Service in Peace and War* (New York: Harper and Brothers, 1948), p. 584.

7. United States Department of State, p. 6.

8. Joseph Persico, *Nuremberg: Infamy on Trial* (New York: Viking Penguin, 1994), p. 7.

9. Gregory Caldeira, "Robert H. Jackson," in Kermit Hall, ed., *Oxford Companion to the Supreme Court of the United States* (New York: Oxford University Press, 1992), p. 444.

10. *TMWC*, vol. I, pp. 11–20.

11. Robert H. Jackson, *The Nuernberg Case* (New York: Alfred A. Knopf, 1947), p. vi.

12. Robert H. Jackson, *Report to the International Conference on Military Trials, London 1945* (Washington, D.C.: Government Printing Office, 1949), p. 299.

13. Ibid., p. 335.

14. *TMWC*, vol. I, p. 95.

15. Jackson, *Report to the International Conference*, p. 330.

16. Ibid., p. 422.

17. Ibid., p. 107.

18. Ibid., p. 115.

19. Ibid., p. 303.

20. *TMWC*, vol. I, p. 11.

21. Office of the United States Chief of Counsel for Prosecution of Axis Criminality, *Nazi Conspiracy and Aggression* (Washington, D.C.: Government Printing Office, 1946), p. 366.

22. *TMWC*, vol. III, p. 527.

23. *TMWC*, vol. IV, pp. 243–244.

Chapter 3. Assembling the Cast for the Trial

1. *Trial of the Major War Criminals Before the International Military Tribunal, Nuremberg, November 14, 1945–October 1, 1946* (Nuremberg: International Military Tribunal, 1947), vol. I, p. 171.

2. Eugene Davidson, *The Trial of the Germans* (New York: Macmillan, 1966), p. 541; *TMWC*, vol. XVII, pp. 229–230.

3. Burton C. Andrus, *I Was the Nuremberg Jailer* (New York: Tower Publications, 1970), pp. 23–24.

4. Ibid., p. 27.

5. Richard Dunlop, *Donovan: America's Master Spy* (Chicago: Rand McNally & Co., 1982), p. 480.

6. Ibid., p. 481.

7. Joseph Persico, *Nuremberg: Infamy on Trial* (New York: Viking Penguin, 1994), p. 119.

8. Robert H. Jackson, "Introduction" in Whitney R. Harris, *Tyranny on Trial: The Evidence at Nuremberg* (Dallas: Southern Methodist University Press, 1954), p. xxxvi.

9. Dunlop, p. 536.

10. Ibid., p. 483.

11. Davidson, p. 122.

12. William J. Donovan, *Nuremberg Trial Transcripts and Documents*, Collection of Cornell Law Library, Ithaca, New York.

13. Davidson, pp. 225–226.

14. Ibid., p. 227.

15. *TMWC*, vol. XII, p. 583.

16. Ibid.

17. *TMWC*, vol. IV, p. 273.

18. Ibid.

19. *TMWC*, vol. XXXIX, pp. 128–129.

20. *TMWC*, vol. VII, p. 366.

21. Office of United States Chief Counsel for the Prosecution of Axis Criminality, *Nazi Conspiracy and Aggression* (Washington, D.C.: Government Printing Office, 1946), vol. VII, p. 974.

22. Davidson, p. 352.

23. Andrus, p. 78.

Chapter 4. Setting the Stage for the Trial

1. Whitney Harris, *Tyranny on Trial: The Evidence at Nuremberg* (Dallas: Southern Methodist University Press, 1954), pp. 27–28.

2. Dan van der Vat, *The Good Nazi: The Life and Lies of Albert Speer* (Boston: Houghton Mifflin Company, 1997), pp. 250–251.

3. Joseph Persico, *Nuremberg: Infamy on Trial* (New York: Viking Penguin, 1994), p. 55.

4. van der Vat, p. 252.

5. Leo Kahn, *Nuremberg Trials* (New York: Ballantine Books, 1972), p. 63.

6. Ibid.

7. Ibid.

8. Ibid.

9. Ibid.

10. G. M. Gilbert, *Nuremberg Diary* (New York: Farrar, Straus, and Company, 1947), p. 6.

11. Kahn, p. 5.

12. Gilbert, p. 7.

13. Ibid., p. 5.

14. Ibid., p. 6.

15. Kahn, p. 63.

16. Persico, p. 97.

17. Gilbert, pp. 20–21.

18. Ibid., p. 131.

19. van der Vat, p. 253.

20. Ibid.

21. Ibid., p. 248.

Chapter 5. The Case for the Prosecution

1. *Trial of the Major War Criminals Before the International Military Tribunal, Nuremberg, November 14,*

1945–October 1, 1946 (Nuremberg: International Military Tribunal, 1947), vol. II, p. 30.

2. Ibid., vol. XXXVIII, p. 191.

3. Robert H. Jackson, "Opening Statement for the United States of America," in Office of United States Chief Counsel for Prosecution of Axis Criminality, *Nazi Conspiracy and Aggression* (Washington, D.C.: Government Printing Office, 1946, vol. I, p. 114.

4. Ibid., p. 116.

5. Ibid., p. 117.

6. Ibid., p. 118.

7. Ibid.

8. Ibid., p. 135.

9. Ibid., p. 136.

10. Ibid.

11. Ibid., p. 143.

12. Ibid., pp. 149–152.

13. Ibid., p. 154.

14. Ibid., p. 156.

15. Ibid., p. 165.

16. Ibid., p. 166.

17. Ibid.

18. Kathleen McLaughlin, "Germans Plotted in '40 to Fight U.S., Jackson Charges," *The New York Times*, November 22, 1945, p. 4.

19. Ann and John Tusa, *The Nuremberg Trial* (New York: Atheneum, 1984), p. 103.

20. G. M. Gilbert, *Nuremberg Diary* (New York: Farrar, Straus and Company, 1947), p. 46.

21. Ibid., p. 49.

22. Ibid., pp. 45–46.

23. *TMWC*, vol. V, pp. 332–333.

24. *TMWC*, vol. III, pp. 565–567.

25. *TMWC*, vol. XIX, pp. 609–610.

26. Office of the United States Chief Counsel for the Prosecution of Axis Criminality, *Nazi Conspiracy and Aggression* (Washington, D.C.: Government Printing Office, 1946), vol. IV, p. 892.

27. Ibid., p. 902.

28. *TMWC*, vol. IV, p. 371.

29. *TMWC*, vol. XI, pp. 330–334.

30. Ibid., p. 335.

31. Tusa, pp. 167–168.

32. Ibid., p. 170.

33. *TMWC*, vol. III, p. 104.

34. Ibid., p. 143.

35. Ibid., p. 144.

36. *TMWC*, vol. VII. p. 850.

37. Ibid.

38. Office of the United States Chief Counsel for the Prosecution of Axis Criminality, vol. I, p. 398.

39. Ibid., p. 400.

40. *TMWC*, vol. V, p. 373.

41. Ibid.

42. Office of the United States Chief Counsel for the Prosecution of Axis Criminality, Appendix A, p. 420.

43. *TMWC*, vol. V, p. 171.

44. *TMWC*, vol. XX, pp. 545–547.

45. *TMWC*, vol. IV, p. 272.

46. *TMWC*, vol. VI, pp. 137–138.

47. Ibid., p. 212.

48. *TMWC*, vol. VIII, p. 42.

49. *TMWC*, vol. III, p. 422.

50. Ibid., p. 418.

51. *TMWC*, vol. VII, pp. 412–414.

52. *TMWC*, vol. IV, p. 477.

53. Whitney R. Harris, *Tyranny on Trial: The Evidence at Nuremberg* (Dallas: Southern Methodist University Press, 1954), p. 350.

54. *TMWC*, vol. IV, pp. 337–338.

55. Tusa, p. 197.

Chapter 6. The Case for the Defense

1. *Trial of the Major War Criminals Before the International Military Tribunal, Nuremberg, November 14, 1945–October 1, 1946* (Nuremberg: International Military Tribunal, 1947), vol. IX, p. 87.

2. Ibid., p. 128.

3. Ibid., p. 479.

4. Ibid., p. 481.

5. Ibid., p. 482.

6. Ibid., p. 401.

7. Ibid., p. 311.

8. Leo Kahn, *Nuremberg Trials* (New York: Ballantine Books, 1972), p. 83.

9. *TMWC*, vol. IX, p. 178.

10. Ibid., p. 354.

11. Ibid., p. 351.

12. Ibid., p. 538.

13. Ibid., p. 431.

14. Ibid., p. 508.

15. Ibid., pp. 511–512.

16. Ibid., p. 538.

17. Ibid., p. 519.

18. Kahn, p. 75.

19. *TMWC*, vol. IX, p. 581.

20. Ibid., p. 614.

21. Ibid., p. 617.

22. Ibid., p. 619.

23. Ibid., vol. X, p. 471.

24. Ibid., p. 626.

25. Ibid., p. 545.

26. Ibid., p. 643.

27. Ibid.

28. Ibid., p. 644.

29. G. M. Gilbert, *Nuremberg Diary* (New York: Farrar, Straus, and Company, 1947), p. 244.

30. Ibid., p. 245.

31. *TMWC*, vol. IX, p. 693.

32. Gilbert, p. 220.

33. *TMWC*, vol. X, pp. 93, 104.

34. Ibid., p. 129.

35. Ibid., p. 135.

36. Ibid., pp. 186–187.

37. Ibid., p. 409.

38. Ibid., pp. 411–412.

39. Gilbert, pp. 230–231.

40. *TMWC*, vol. XI, p. 252.

41. *TMWC*, vol. IV, p. 386.

42. Ibid., p. 381.

43. *TMWC*, vol. XI, pp. 322–323.

44. Ibid., p. 339.

45. Ibid., p. 243.

46. Deborah Dwork and Joan van Pelt, "The Politics of a Strategy for Auschwitz-Birkenau," *Cardozo Law Review*, December 1998, vol. 20, p. 687.

47. Ibid., p. 416.

48. Ibid., p. 417.

49. Gilbert, p. 259.

50. *TMWC*, vol. XIII, p. 278.

51. *TMWC*, vol. V, pp. 227–228.

52. *TMWC*, vol. XVII, pp. 378–380.

53. *TMWC*, vol. XXII, p. 390.

54. Ibid., p. 396.

55. Ibid., pp. 366–368.

Chapter 7. The Judges Decide

1. Francis Biddle papers, Syracuse University Library, Syracuse, New York, box 14, "Notes on Judgement," pp. 2–3.

2. Ibid., box 1, "Correspondence," p. 46.

3. Ibid., box 14, "Notes on Judgment," p. 12.

4. Ibid., pp. 17–18.

5. Ibid., p. 19.

6. Ibid., pp. 35–36.

7. *Trial of the Major War Criminals Before the International Military Tribunal, Nuremberg, November 14, 1945–October 1, 1946* (Nuremberg: International Military Tribunal, 1947), vol. I, p. 225.

8. Biddle, box 14, "Notes on Judgment," p. 38.

9. Ibid., p. 6.

10. Ibid., p. 7.

11. Ibid., box 5, "Defendant Memos," p. 71.

12. Ibid.

13. Ibid., box 14, "Notes on Judgement," p. 10.

14. Ibid., p. 29.

15. Ibid., p. 24.

16. Ibid., pp. 44–56.

17. Ibid., pp. 38, 55.

18. Ibid., p. 28.

19. Ibid., pp. 59–63.

20. Telford Taylor, *The Anatomy of the Nuremberg Trials* (New York: Alfred A. Knopf, 1992), p. 562.

21. Ibid., p. 365.

22. Dan van der Vat, *The Good Nazi: The Life and Lies of Albert Speer* (Boston: Houghton Mifflin Company, 1997), p. 249.

23. Ibid., p. 241.

24. Biddle, box 5, "Defendant Memos," p. 339; Bradley F. Smith, *Reaching Judgement at Nuremberg* (New York: Basic Books, 1977), pp. 218–220.

25. Biddle, box 14, "Notes on Judgment," p. 57.

26. TMWC, vol. I, pp. 171–341.

27. Ibid., p. 226.

28. Ibid., pp. 270–274.

29. Ibid., pp. 275–278.

30. G. M. Gilbert, *Nuremberg Diary* (New York: Farrar, Straus and Company, 1947), pp. 431–433.

31. Smith, p. 298.

32. Taylor, pp. 601–607.

33. Kingsbury Smith, "The Execution of Nazi War Criminals," October 16, 1946, <http://users.deltanet.com/~cybrgbl/nuremberg/nuremberg.html> (November 11, 1999).

34. Burton C. Andrus, *I Was the Nuremberg Jailer* (New York: Tower Publications, 1970), p. 162.

35. Smith, pp. 301–302.

36. David J. Sheffer, "U.S. Policy on International Criminal Tribunals," October 21, 1998, <http://www.state.gov/www/policyremarks/1998/980331_sheffer_tribs.html> (May 15, 1999).

37. Ibid.

38. "U.S. Statement Before the U.N. General Assembly Sixth Committee," October 21, 1999 <http://www.igc.org/icc/html/us19991021.html> (November 11, 1999).

39. International Criminal Tribunal for the Former Yugoslavia, "Fact Sheet," October 27, 1999 <http://www.un.org/icyt/glance/ fact.htm> (November 11, 1999).

Glossary

Allies—Great Britain, France, United States, the Soviet Union, and many smaller countries that joined together during World War II.

Axis—Germany, Italy, and later Japan in World War II.

concentration camps—Prison camps for prisoners in Nazi Germany and occupied territories during World War II. These camps later became known as sites of mass murder of inmates.

conspiracy—A secret plan by two or more people to commit a crime or do harm.

court martial—The process of putting members of the armed forces on trial.

crimes against humanity—Acts such as murder, forced relocation, enslavement, and extermination of people for political, racial, or religious reasons.

criminal trial—The hearing of evidence by a court that decides whether a person or organization accused of a crime is guilty or innocent.

defendant—The person or organization accused of a crime during a trial.

dissenting opinion—An opinion written by a judge who disagrees with the majority of justices on the court.

ex post facto law—A law that makes punishable an act that was not a crime when that act was committed. Such a law is generally forbidden.

Geneva Conventions—A series of international agreements between 1846 and 1949 to lessen the harm done to fighters and civilians by war.

genocide—The deliberate extermination of a people or a nation.

indictment—Formal charges of a crime.

jurisdiction—The legal authority of a court to hear a certain type of case.

opinion—A formal statement presented by a court.

precedent—All of the prior laws or decisions on an issue that is presently before a court.

tribunal—A court of justice.

war crimes—Acts, such as murdering civilians or forcing them to perform slave labor, that violate the international laws of war.

Further Reading

Altman, Linda Jacobs. *Genocide: The Systematic Killing of a People.* Springfield, N.J.: Enslow Publishers, Inc., 1995.

———. *The Holocaust Ghettos.* Springfield, N.J.: Enslow Publishers, Inc., 1998.

———. *The Holocaust, Hitler, and Nazi Germany.* Berkeley Heights, N.J.: Enslow Publishers, Inc., 1999.

Beyers, Ann. *The Holocaust Overview.* Springfield, N.J.: Enslow Publishers, Inc., 1998.

———. *The Holocaust Camps.* Springfield, N.J.: Enslow Publishers, Inc., 1998.

Fremon, David K. *The Holocaust Heroes.* Springfield, N.J.: Enslow Publishers, Inc., 1998.

Gaskin, Hilary. *Eyewitness at Nuremberg.* London: Arms and Armour, 1990.

Gay, Kathlyn. *Neo-Nazis: A Growing Threat.* Springfield, N.J.: Enslow Publishers, Inc., 1997.

Persico, Joseph E. *Nuremberg: Infamy on Trial.* New York: Viking Penguin, 1994.

Stein, R. Conrad. *World War II in Europe: "America Goes to War."* Hillside, N.J.: Enslow Publishers, Inc., 1994.

Strahinich, Helen. *The Holocaust: Understanding and Remembering.* Springfield, N.J.: Enslow Publishers, Inc., 1996.

Taylor, Telford. *The Anatomy of the Nuremberg Trials.* New York: Alfred A. Knopf, 1992.

van der Vat, Dan. *The Good Nazi: The Life and Lies of Albert Speer.* Boston: Houghton Mifflin, 1997.

Yeatts, Tabatha. *The Holocaust Survivors.* Springfield, N.J.: Enslow Publishers, Inc., 1998.

Internet Addresses

International Criminal Tribunal for the Former Yugoslavia, "Fact Sheet"
  <http://www.un.org/icty/glance/procfact-e.htm>

"The Execution of Nazi War Criminals" by Kingsbury Smith
  <http://www.law.umkc.edu/faculty/projects/ftrials/nuremberg/NurembergNews10_16_46.html>

Atlantic Unbound "Nuremberg Revisited"
  <http://www.theatlantic.com/unbound/flashbks/nurember/nurem.htm>

U.S. Holocaust Memorial Museum, "The Holocaust: A Learning Site for Students"
  <http://www.ushmm.org/outreach/>

The Jewish Student Online Research Center (JSOURCE), "The Nuremberg Trials: The Defendants and Verdicts" by Ben S. Austin
  <http://www.us-israel.org/jsource/Holocaust/verdicts.html>

The Holocaust\Shoah Page
  <http://www.mtsu.edu/~baustin/holo.html>

Index